IBSEN AND THE TEMPER OF
NORWEGIAN LITERATURE

IBSEN AND THE TEMPER OF NORWEGIAN LITERATURE

JAMES WALTER McFARLANE

OCTAGON BOOKS

A DIVISION OF FARRAR, STRAUS AND GIROUX

New York   1979

Reprinted 1979
by special arrangement with Oxford University Press

OCTAGON BOOKS
A DIVISION OF FARRAR, STRAUS & GIROUX, INC.
19 Union Square West
New York, N.Y. 10003

Library of Congress Cataloging in Publication Data

McFarlane, James Walter.

    Ibsen and the temper of Norwegian literature.
    Reprint of the ed. published by Oxford University Press, London, New York.
    Bibliography: p.
    Includes index.
    1. Norwegian literature—19th century—History and criticism.
    2. Norwegian literature—20th century—History and criticism.
    I. Title.
[PT8435.M3   1979]   839.8′2′09   79-195
ISBN 0-374-95479-8

Printed in USA by
Thomson-Shore, Inc.
Dexter, Michigan

CONTENTS

ACKNOWLEDGEMENTS AND THANKS

The chapters on Holberg, Ibsen and Bjørnson make use of material that has previously appeared in *The Times Literary Supplement*; the chapter on Kielland was first published as an article in *The Norseman*; a large part of the Hamsun chapter originally appeared (with supporting footnote references) in the Publications of the Modern Language Association of America, *PMLA*; for permission to use this material, I am indebted to the editors and proprietors of the publications mentioned.

My grateful thanks are also due to a number of institutions and individuals who have helped in various ways: to the Office of Cultural Relations, Oslo, and the Norwegian–British North Sea Foundation, Oslo, for financial assistance that allowed me to spend six months in residence in Oslo working on the book; to the Council of King's College, Newcastle upon Tyne for granting me the necessary leave of absence; to my colleagues in the Department of German and Scandinavian Studies there; to the staffs of King's College Library, Newcastle, and the University Library, Oslo; and to Mr. Carl Hambro, sometime Cultural Counsellor, Royal Norwegian Embassy, London.

J.W.McF.

King's College,
University of Durham,
Newcastle upon Tyne.

✱ 1 ✱

INTRODUCTION

Like Darwin and Karl Marx and the Rev. W. A. Spooner,
Henrik Ibsen lent his name for the enrichment of the English
dictionary; and in sponsoring a new 'ism', he at once suffered
himself to be both better and worse known than he would otherwise have been. His name, in the early days, held an invitation to
identify him as the source of something expounded or dis-
seminated—perhaps even perpetrated, since in his case his
adherents were not 'ists' but also 'ites', with all the subtle force
of opprobrium that that exerts. His work, one feels, could so
easily have become something one had opinions about rather
than familiarity with, as Marxism is a known thing to many for
whom *Das Kapital* remains a closed book, or as *The Origin of
Species* is taken as read. He ran the danger of being saddled with
that dubious distinction for a creative artist—of becoming, as
was said of Freud, 'no more a person . . . but a whole climate of
opinion'. Yet this was not what happened.

He began, in the England of the 1890s, conspicuously, wring-
ing from the public a cry of outraged purity, one of those cries
which—as Henry James once put it—'have so often and so
pathetically resounded through the Anglo-Saxon world'. He provoked *Punch* into making elaborate fun of him, and shocked the
Sporting and Dramatic into scandalized appeals to the authorities.
In the years that followed, a great many people looked him up
and down: Havelock Ellis hailed him as a great liberator;
Professor Saintsbury bludgeoned him with phrases of awful
finality, crying: 'He is parochial, and not of a very large or distinguished parish. He is, in that parish, a frequenter chiefly of
the hospital and the asylum.' W. B. Yeats sniffed him and smelt

only what he called 'the stale odour of spilt poetry'; D. H. Lawrence took one look and waved him away as one of 'the intellectual hopeless people'; Virginia Woolf detected a luminous transparency in his realism; and Ezra Pound pronounced him all for the good. He has been Peoples Theatred and Shaftesbury Avenued, he has been Extra-Muralled and Third Programmed and Paper Backed; his translated plays have been awarded settlers' rights, sometimes to the extent of giving them a Scottish milieu instead of a Norwegian one; he himself has been granted 'naturalization by syllabus' following the action of at least two of our Universities in pronouncing him a proper and examinable part of Eng.Lit.; he has been known to masquerade in the provincial press as Henry Gibson. He whom Shaw once interpreted to a select Fabian audience in the St. James's Restaurant is now transmitted on television to the firesides of the nation; he who was once vilified as the agent of widespread moral agitation is now considered suitable for peak-hour, Sunday-evening viewing. His works and his letters and his draft manuscripts have been made accessible in translation to an extent few other foreigners have enjoyed. For over seventy years he has been written up, written down and written off, during which time he has thriven equally on the abuse of the righteous and the eulogy of the misguided. By giving him the full treatment, we have made an Englishman of him as thoroughly as ever the Germans made Shakespeare German.

The temptation for those who, of Norwegian literature, know only him is doubtless to think of the rest of it as being in some way rather like Ibsen writ small. It is true that Ibsen is genuinely and essentially Norwegian; true also that the ties linking his drama with his native land are close and intimate, so that the meaning of the plays yields itself in all its full richness only when they are interpreted within the context of a Norwegian milieu; yet the fact remains that he is not typical. To suppose that the Norwegian mode of literature consists in trying to give expression to the kind of Norwegian-ness that Ibsen's works so splendidly and uniquely embody is mistaken—Ibsen adorns Norwegian literature, but he does not exemplify it.

Time and space, the ravages of history and the burdens of geography have left their trace on the features of Norway's literature. In a country precariously balanced on the top of Europe, cut across by fjord and ravine and gorge, monstrously furrowed into mountain and valley, the tradition of living was for long centuries one of multiple isolation: national, cultural, individual. Banished for a whole epoch to a shadowy corner of history, the country remained a collection of small, scattered communities, remote pockets in a land already itself remote, products of a sternly contoured landscape which imposed on each valley and each coastal inlet an involuntary independence. Individuality—of temperament, of custom, of dialect—retained its original sharp and rugged outlines, for the social intercourse was never on the kind of scale to allow these things to rub themselves against each other into smooth conformity. Local, limited allegiance to the family and to the valley has always been strong and comparatively undemonstrative; national loyalty, on the other hand, for men so instinctively hostile to any hint of superimposed uniformity, seems more like a fierce act of will, something the ardour of which needs to be demonstrated by deed and proclaimed by word. One is still conscious of the operation of these factors today, even though much of the old way of life has been overlaid by newer conditions of living that followed Norway's re-emergence in the nineteenth century as an influential force in European and world affairs; independence and individuality and resourcefulness are still characteristic even in a society where the more obvious historical and geographical isolation has been broken down by political action and the spread of modern communications.

Common to this life and the literature that relates to it is a reverence for action, for conspicuous achievement, for vigorous accomplishment. Word and deed substitute for each other with astonishing facility: if it had been left to Ibsen to choose an epitaph for Bjørnson, he would have said 'His life was his best poem'; and when Bjørnson in turn paid tribute to Nansen, he remarked that although he (Bjørnson) had written the National Anthem 'Yes, we love this country', Nansen had lived it. Poetry

is commended as deed in thought, deed as poetry in action—so
that when literature comes up for appreciation, there is a strong
compulsion to judge it by reference to its effectiveness as an
undertaking, to ponder its practical achievement as a surrogate
for action in the promotion of human welfare and the enrichment
of daily living.

It is not suggested that there is anything improper in this.
Only that when assumptions of this kind about the nature and
purpose of poetry combine with an urgent love of country and a
jealousy for its rank and reputation among the nations, unexpected things begin to happen, and happen to Ibsen in particular.
Some of his countrymen, including critics of repute and distinction, are ready to support the idea that because Ibsen was in a
number of respects not typically or enthusiastically Norwegian,
because he failed to epitomize the Norwegian spirit (or what one
sets up ideally as that spirit), that therefore his greatness is somehow to be marked down. Something of this could be remarked
not long ago when the then Professor of Scandinavian Literature
at the University of Oslo held a speech at the unveiling of a statue
to Bjørnstjerne Bjørnson at Molde, in the course of which he put
the question: 'Who was the greatest Norwegian?' Bearing in
mind the special piety the occasion demanded, one realizes that in
the circumstances only one answer was possible; but in showing
his working, in thinking his preliminary thoughts out aloud, the
speaker is reported to have drawn up a short-list of four names:
Saint Olav, Henrik Wergeland, Bjørnstjerne Bjørnson, and Fridtjof
Nansen. To eliminate Ibsen from the first four, especially when
the list includes two other authors, seems incredible to anybody
outside Norway; even when one makes full allowance for its being
a thoroughly Bjørnsonian occasion with all that that means for
Ibsen's name, it is still not easy for an outsider to comprehend.
Is the logic of it that, because with some degree of truth it could
be argued that Ibsen was not Norwegianly great, it follows he
was not one of the greatest Norwegians?

At least the two attitudes to Ibsen briefly noted here serve to
bracket him, the one falling short, the other going too far; and
truth is straddled. It is largely as a commentary to this, a com-

mentary on the relationship between Ibsen and the national tradition in literature to which he belongs that these studies are intended. They assume that the traffic is two-way: that any account of Norwegian literature in modern times must be prepared to allot a central place to Ibsen if meaning and perspective are to be given to the whole; and that, conversely, one's understanding of Ibsen is enhanced by seeing his work in the context of his own national literature. There is no suggestion that these separate essays could by any kind of arithmetic add up to a literary history. The original intention was that only those authors should qualify for inclusion who fulfilled two conditions: one, that they were already accessible, at least in some measure, in English translation; and, two, that they were of such stature that they could properly claim more than merely domestic importance. These principles have in the last resort not been strictly adhered to; and once exceptions had been made, for example in the case of Obstfelder or Vesaas (both largely inaccessible in English), then good and convincing arguments could well be advanced on behalf of many other authors of ability and importance who are in the same position: Hans Kinck or Olaf Bull or Nordahl Grieg or Johan Falkberget, to mention only a few. It should also go on record that the choice of authors in this volume has done less than justice to Norway's lyric poets; it would be wholly false to conclude from the present selection that the genius of Norwegian literature is preponderantly dramatic and narrative and only insignificantly lyric; a literary *history* for the student would soon show the truth, whereas the present volume, being meant for what Newman once called 'the educated but unlearned public', is distorted in this dimension by the comparative wealth of translated novel and drama and the paucity of translated lyric.

★ 2 ★

LUDVIG HOLBERG

Ludvig Holberg had no predecessors in Scandinavia, no other shoulders to stand on, nobody to help with the rough. Those years which it might seem proper for an Englishman to call 'the silver age'—from the civil wars until well into the eighteenth century—are commonly written off in the domestic histories of Danish and Norwegian literature as 'det lærde tidsrum', the period of pedantry and barren learning, an epoch when the language was strong but ungainly and threatening to become muscle-bound after its efforts to cope with philosophy and science, an empty trough—empty, that is, until Holberg abundantly and triumphantly filled it.

Admittedly, his work is not without unevenness. There is none of the sleek finish of Voltaire, none of the high gloss of Pope, both of them contemporaries of his with whom it is possible in one aspect or another to compare him; they were fortunate in being able to work for much of their time with a finishing touch, operating within a tradition of sophistication and with a language already refined; Holberg was labourer and craftsman in one, and his work has that slightly tacky look that even the most skilful cannot avoid when materials of less than the highest quality are used on an unprimed surface. As the creator of a literary language and the founder of a literary tradition, he, more than most, demands to be judged within his historical context; and it is here, rather than in any intrinsic deficiencies, that the reason is to be sought why a man of his stature, a man who was all things to Scandinavian literature, should have attracted less than his proper measure of attention from the rest of Europe.

There can be no denying his domestic importance. From the

time of his first *succès de scandale*, the publication in 1719 of the mock-heroic poem *Peder Paars*, until his death in 1754, he dominated the world of Scandinavian letters; his influence since that day on what one must, in deference to national passions, cautiously call the Dano–Norwegian cultural area has been so immense and so pervasive that its extent cannot even be guessed at; it is unthinkable, to say the least, that Danish and Norwegian literature could ever have developed as it did without him. Although he wrought no miracles of inventive genius, the fecundity of his comic inspiration is astonishing. When invited in 1722 to contribute to the repertoire of the newly-established Danish theatrical company in Copenhagen, he turned out comedies faster than the company could rehearse and stage them: fifteen plays in as many months made up his first consignment, among them *The Political Tinker, Jeppe of the Hill, Erasmus Montanus* and others that belong to his very best work. By the end of four and a half years, the toll of comedies had risen to twenty-five; in all he completed thirty-four plays,[1] seven of which belong to the last few years of his life. The sheer speed at which he worked was in itself enough to start the suspicion that not everything was the result of independent inspiration; and there has grown up around his name a luxuriance of minute scholarship, cataloguing his indebtedness, his borrowings, his plagiarisms, listing the recognizable bits of Terence and Plautus and Regnard and Molière, the pickings from Spanish and Low

[1] They are, in roughly chronological order: *The Political Tinker (Den politiske Kandestøber); The Weathercock (Den Vægelsindede); Jean de France; Jeppe of the Hill (Jeppe paa Bjerget); The Talkative Barber (Mester Gert Westphaler); Jacob von Tyboe; The Fussy Man (Den Stundesløse); Erasmus Montanus; Don Ranudo de Colibrados; The Maternity Room (Barselstuen); Ulysses von Ithacia; Without Head or Tail (Uden Hoved og Hale); Witchcraft, or False Alarm (Hexeri eller Blind Allarm); Melampe; Eleventh of June (Den 11. Juni); The Arabian Powder (Det arabiske Pulver); The Christmas Party (Julestuen); Masquerade (Mascarade); Journey to a Spring (Kilderejsen); Diderich Menschenschreck; Henrich and Pernille (Henrich og Pernille); The lucky Shipwreck (Det lykkelige Skibbrud); The invisible ones (De Usynlige); The Peasant in Pawn (Den pantsatte Bondedreng); Pernille's brief Maidenhood (Pernilles korte Frøkenstand); Social Ambition (Den honette Ambition); The Funeral of Danish Drama (Den danske Komedies Ligbegængelse); Plutus; Sganarel's Journey to the Land of the Philosophers (Sganarels Rejse til det filosofiske Land); Abracadabra; Self-supposed Philosopher (Philosophus udi egen Indbildning); The Changed Bridegroom (Den forvandlede Brudgom); Artaxerxes; The Republic (Republiqven).*

German and English sources, taunting him when hostile with the nickname 'Plautiberg', honouring him when sympathetic with the title 'Molière of the North'. After these few years packed with dramatic authorship, he turned to more scholarly work, and between 1729 and 1742 he published among other things his *Description of Denmark and Norway (Dannemarks og Norges Beskrivelse*, 1729), *History of the Kingdom of Denmark (Dannemarks Riges Historie*, 1732–35), *Synopsis historiæ universalis* (1733), *Description of Bergen (Bergens Beskrivelse*, 1737), *General Church History (Almindelig Kirkehistorie*, 1738) and *History of the Jews (Jødiske Historie*, 1742). And if, in the thirty-odd dramas, he is the Molière, he is in *Peder Paars* the Boileau and Cervantes, in his *Epistles (Epistler*, 1748–54) the Montaigne; his novel *Niels Klim* (originally in Latin) is the *Gulliver's Travels*, and his *Moral Thoughts (Moralske Tanker*, 1744) a Danish *Spectator*. As dramatist, satirist, essayist, historian and popular philosopher he left an abiding mark, and although posterity has hesitated to admit him to the class of Great Europeans, he was by any international standards great and in his outlook profoundly European.

In later life, it amused him to pretend that his Europeanism began with the geographical accident of his birth-place; he was born in 1684, in Bergen, a Noah's Ark of a place, as he called it, inhabited by all manner of creatures and full of a cosmopolitan spirit. Certainly, whatever else was achieved, it marks the start of a battle of national pride: Bergen the town of his birth and Norway the land of his youth being forever ranged against Copenhagen and Denmark, his *Wahlheimat*, in the struggle to claim Holberg as their own. And yet it is surely in his education, an education owing less to formal instruction than to independent intellectual foraging, that we must seek the really formative influences that gave him his breadth of mind; he raided the great libraries of Western Europe like a man with a great hunger. Two accomplishments carried him far, both socially and geographically: a facility in languages and skill on the flute. In Oxford, where he studied from 1706 to 1708, he was well liked on many high tables as a genial and witty conversationalist, and his assistance often welcomed in the making of music; but in his life as in his comedies there was behind it all a serious intent, for his social graces were also his bread and butter, and Oxford was not the first nor was it to be the last time he supported himself and financed his studies by giving language and music lessons. And always it was the libraries—the Bodleian, the Bibliothèque Mazarine, the Vatican—that seemed to be pulling him. His life until he was past thirty was a studious vagabondage; his travels, as often as not on foot, sent him ranging far over Europe and deep into her cultural heritage; from Holland and England, from France and Italy and Germany he brought back a rich plunder of ideas. In this acquisitive and receptive way he was *of* Europe to a degree approached by no other of his European contemporaries. Here was a man who, as Brandes put it, opened doors, who flung wide the windows on the stuffy atmosphere of Danish provincialism and thereby put all Scandinavia in his debt. And it is no discredit to him, it may be added, if one admits that little emerged to attract the attention of contemporary Europe but the boisterous noise of a family putting its own house in order.

Nothing could be more misleading than the rhetorical question put by William Archer in the course of his address to the Anglo-Danish Society of Copenhagen in 1924: 'Is it not,' he asked, 'that Holberg the moralist was a slight, perfunctory, almost negligible appendix to Holberg the artist?' In the wider context of rebuttal of which this forms part, Archer was unquestionably right; Holberg's comedies are in no sense political tracts, and to interpret *Jeppe of the Hill* as a piece of anti-revolutionary propaganda, a prophetic piece of anti-Communism, is sheer silliness. But Archer was not content to knock down a particularly grotesque Aunt Sally; he was confident he knew how the real Holberg had worked, and the picture he draws is of one submitting obediently to a pure and uncontaminated inspiration, serving no end but Art itself, oblivious to everything but an inner urge to create immortal dramatic characters; only then, Archer goes on: 'when the portrait was completed, with an accuracy of design and a depth of colouring worthy of Rembrandt, the painter yielded to the conventional demand for a copybook moral and threw off the first, the most obvious that came into his head.' To pretend that

2

the moral element is merely a tiny excrescence on the fair features of his creative genius, a parasitical growth that a piece of simple surgery might remove, is however completely to misrepresent the cast of Holberg's mind and the nature of his work. The didacticism there is not something stuck on; there is no mere clipping together of entertainment and instruction; the moral is there not as a pill is in its sugar but as a meaning is in the symbol, as something inherent, something at one with that which expresses it. History, satire, and drama—indeed all the things that came from his pen—were not merely the occasions for moralizing but the indispensable media. Creative passion and moral inspiration were in him indivisibly; and it is false to imagine that either lends itself easily to independent evaluation.

In one of his more scholarly works published in 1716, before his career as a creative writer had begun, he arranged the separate intellectual disciplines within a hierarchy of values, rising from logic and metaphysics (which for a time he professed but also, in the form in which they were then generally practised, utterly despised), and classical philology (which he also professed but considered almost equally worthless), through history, mathematics, natural science and medicine, to its culmination in moral philosophy, 'whereby the mind is cultivated and Man is as it were formed'. The supremacy of moral thinking over all other intellectual activities held good for him for the rest of his life, his mind was at all times dominated by it, and a few years before his death, in the preface to the *Epistles*, he summed up the endeavour of the past three decades:

With this latest work I have in some degree completed my purpose of moralizing by all available means; and the Reader himself must judge which method might be considered most effective. The different means of which I have availed myself are those of comic *poëmata*, of satires, of reflections on the exploits of Heroes and Heroines, of serious moral thoughts, of fictitious travel books, and finally that of these Epistles; so that there only remains the development of moral themes in dialogue form, a thing which might nevertheless be said to have occurred in my plays, which consist of dialogue and which are almost all of them moral.

Thus was his work tethered. Whereas Shaw was by his own con-

LUDVIG HOLBERG   19

fession a specialist in immoral plays, and Holberg in moral ones, yet their motives were identical; and when Shaw wrote: 'I write plays with the deliberate object of converting the nation to my opinions. . . . I have no other object in writing plays', Holberg would surely have nodded his agreement. All forms of writing serve the same purpose, the universal betterment (as he conceived it) of mankind; as literary forms, for him they differ from each other only in their respective degrees of effectiveness.

At no point, however, is he systematic. What Kierkegaard said of Lessing is applicable to him in almost equal measure: that he did not permit himself to be deceived into being 'world historic' and systematic, but submitted everything to a delicately poised subjectivity. In spite of his encyclopaedic knowledge of the ideas current in Europe during his day (in which he also resembled Lessing), he was not disposed to admit any system as having overriding authority. His moral judgements, products though they were of a richly informed mind, were instinctive and owed their origin ultimately to nothing so much as a sturdy sense of disbelief. Like Swift, he had an ingrained mistrust of the accepted thing; and of his work too it might be said, as it has been said of Swift's, that it keeps commanding: 'It is not as you think—look!' But there the comparison must end; for whilst Swift used his gifts as a scalpel to 'inspect beyond the Surface and the Rind of Things', cutting through outward appearances and penetrating deep, Holberg has the hands of a conjurer rather than a surgeon. He sets before us familiar things, makes a pass with his supple fingers, and there to our delight they are revealed standing grotesquely on their heads; but we are not allowed to disperse without the bewildered feeling that possibly things would look odder still if they were set back on their feet again.

A moral dilemma, it has been said, first presents itself to us as the question of what we ought to *do*, but that it inevitably transforms itself into the question of what we want to *be*; and in this steady drift away from arbitration by a code of principles to the point where we respond to some personal ideal of character which we shape and carry within us is possibly to be sought the formal justification of drama as an instrument of moral persuasion. A shape, however, as others have observed before, can be produced either by plumping out or paring down; and of these two procedures, it is not over-fanciful to see the one tending towards tragedy and the other towards comedy. In Schiller's later tragedies, for example—and Schiller had much to say on the subject of 'the stage as a moral institution'—we seem to start with the bare armature of an ideal, some skeleton vision of the Sublime, to which each successive tragedy adds a positive and elaborative example, urging 'Thus shalt thou act'. But whereas tragedy of this order seems to model, comedy carves; it chips lumps away from an amorphous block of confused ideas, removing what is unwanted. Such is the cumulative effect of Holberg's comedies, and to see them merely as a set of unco-ordinated prohibitions is to see only the chips on the floor and overlook the shape on the bench.

It is then in the nature of things that exemplary ideals can rarely be successfully objectified or personalized in comedy; without the space for manœuvre that tragedy offers, goodness is resistant to dramatic treatment. To put the reasonable alongside the ridiculous, the sensible alongside the outrageous, might admittedly serve to make the discrepancy obvious to all, but only at the risk of blunting the satire with priggishness; it is as difficult to be admirable in comedy as it is easy to be ridiculous, and virtue becomes something to be talked about rather than presented in action. The nearest Holberg ever got to the positive embodiment of virtue—exempting, this is, those figures like the Lieutenant and Baron Nilus who merely comment on rather than enact goodness—was in the creation of Jacob, the brother of Erasmus Montanus; and when Jacob stands up to his conceited brother and says: 'He who studies the most important things has, I think, the most profound learning . . . I study farming and the cultivation of the earth, therefore I am more learned than you, Monsieur', we savour the spectacle of the pedant out-syllogized by shrewd native wit, but we sense the priggishness not very far away. Generally in these dramas, there is little direct dealing with the exemplary or the serious sides of life, no trace of deeper feeling, no shadow of death; but to conclude that there is no depth in him is false. He dealt in terms of the absurd, but as purposefully and responsibly as any classic *reductio ad absurdum*. He drew no neat circle round those aspects of life he approved of; but although the ideal itself remains unrealized, the dramas in their sum compose a kind of commentary to it, the antics of the fools and the gluttons and the windbags, the fops and the hypocrites and the liars serving as a series of tangential strokes which, like those of the mathematician's 'envelope', help to delimit an area, a philosophy of reasonableness, wherein he felt true sanity resided.

The ideal thus encompassed was conservative rather than radical, social rather than ethical, pastoral rather than heroic. Never thin-lipped or cruel, never showing signs of real disgust or anger or of being emotionally involved, he mounted an intellectually distanced offensive against those faults that inhabit the person: complacency, self-ignorance, self-satisfaction, pomposity, pedantry and the *fureur de se distinguer*. It was not in his scheme of things to make war on public injustice or official corruption or abuses in social organization; there is no lashing the knave who unscrupulously seeks money or possessions or worldly power; his business is with the exposure of fools, of those who in insolent stupidity try to impress their fellow-men as being better than they really are. Offence comes with the indulgence in practices, in themselves often unexceptionable, without the requisite ability or talent or money or breeding or position.

An overt emphasis is placed throughout on the doctrine of 'Know thyself'; but there is an equal insistence, less explicit but no less urgent, on the virtues of knowing one's station: of knowing how to leave politics to the politicians, upper class manners to upper class society, elegant living to those with deep purses. Breeding without money, he seems to suggest, is only slightly less ridiculous than money without breeding. Humility and modesty, he assures us, are the marks of true self-awareness and the fruits of self-discipline; but at the same time we are made to feel that there is in operation in any well-ordered society a benevolent system of social checks that saves us from ourselves. As a simple peasant, henpecked by his wife and finding solace in the bottle, Jeppe might not be an admirable figure but he is one that society can at least tolerate; remove the social ballast, make a baron of him, and he becomes bestial and intolerable; cast him down again, sentence him to death, and he becomes a touching figure taking farewell of those simple things in life that had given him pleasure. Our rank in society is not an obstacle to progress but a safeguard against those things we do not really measure up to, a protective device which if suddenly removed might lead to disaster. Our place in life is something we are born to or trained for; professionalism and expert knowledge are conducive to order, the enthusiastic amateur is dangerous. If we are taken down a peg, it is to put us in our proper place, not to punish.

When a comic dramatist invites his audience to share some such unspoken ideal with him, he soon finds himself in a dilemma: his standards must to some extent correlate with existing public opinion, otherwise there is no sharing of them with the audience; but to make them identical leads only to the ridiculing of what everybody in any case despises—there is no moulding of human values, only the reinforcement of those already there, no moral achievement, only a theatrical one. A partial answer to this problem, and one which is not uncommon in Holberg, is to stratify the ridicule. The comic and moral achievement of *Erasmus Montanus* is not exhausted by our witnessing the correction of a conceited and pedantic young man; nor even when we have added the only slightly more oblique criticism directed against the academic mania of Holberg's day for the formalism of empty learning as distinct from true knowledge. Per Degn, the old *academicus* who confounds his learned young rival by reeling off 'Gaudeamus igitur' and a few grammatical catch phrases, has his triumph; but there is still comic censure *via* him of the notion that wisdom is what ordinary folk do not understand. And although old Jeronimus, a sympathetic rather than an utterly ridiculous figure in his bluff and honest ignorance, wins acknowledgement from Erasmus that the world is really flat, he embodies a warning that the common-sense view has often very little to do with truth and that things are not always as they seem.

When we are inclined to criticize Holberg for seeming too ready to yield to the opportunities for easy wit, this is worth recalling; for there is often under the superficialities a subtler campaign to discredit not what was already in disrepute but what was falsely or ignorantly or foolishly respected.

Yet what is it about these dramas, the reader finds himself asking, that seems to contribute both to their strength and to whatever weakness they have? That makes them seem so wilfully and yet so triumphantly deficient? As though they were deliberately one dimension short of what they might have been, supreme in their limitations and yet conveying a sense of potentialities unfulfilled?

Is it that the humour in them is for the most part broad and ample but uncomplicated, that the belly laugh meant more to him than the wry, ambiguous smile? In an age when comedy was beginning to pay court to simpering and sentimental virtue, when the trend that was to lead from Destouches and Marivaux to Nivelle de la Chaussée and the *comédie larmoyante* was already under way, he is conspicuous by reason of a low-brow vein of comedy that was at all times robust, often rumbustious, occasionally scurrilous. Sex ever rears an ugly head, love is a stranger to gallantry, chamber-pot humour is a stand-by; for his peasants, there often seems to be no gesture too gross, no word too obscene. Yet there is little offence; these things are all of a piece with the general style of the comedies, and Holberg was surely right in passionately resisting expurgation, believing that to remove these elements would be to sacrifice much of the freshness and simplicity of the work.

Or is it that the plots, for all their twistings and turnings and luxuriance, always seem to lie within a single plane? Richly intricate in one way, and employing the traditional devices of mistaken identity, contrived misunderstanding, practical joke and all the other conventional apparatus, their intricacy seems nevertheless to be that of surface decoration, of filigree. It is not that the plays are merely innocent of sub-plot, not that they merely lack the make-weight of added complication such as our Restoration dramatists topped up with when they borrowed from Molière; it is simply that in their technique they lack any extras in depth.

Or can it be merely that in modern eyes the characters seem wanting in psychological depth? Their tones and their gestures, the rhythms of their speech and the quality of their manners come admittedly straight from nature and confirm by their wealth of brilliant detail Holberg's close and sympathetic observation of contemporary life; but although they have wit and gaiety and idiom, although their appearance of having stepped straight in off the streets gives them a deceptive air of 'reality', they are life-like rather than living, being wrung from a mind saturated with reading. Whilst Jeronimus and Magdelone speak in genuine accents, whilst Henrich and Pernille and Arv seem completely at home in the servants' quarters of their Danish household, they are nevertheless naturalized foreigners, pioneer settlers; their actions are predictable, their minds run on tracks which by-pass the more familiar realities by which we love and toil and instead run off into the eccentric country of spoof and hoax and stunt, so well mapped by the *commedia dell' arte* and its French imitators. The sluts and the rogues, the hags and the idiots, the man-mad spinsters and the gullible victims of the practical jokes have the strong flat colours of a reproduction; and where their patterns of behaviour are concerned, Holberg has looked it all up in books.

Yet these things in themselves, although they may help to explain, do not fully account for the presence behind all the rompings and the great paraphernalia of plot and character of a curious structural strength that seems bound up in some way with these linear qualities. Expecting from drama some development of action, we find concatenation of incident; expecting mutation of character, we find revelation; when Jeppe falls in a drunken stupor by the roadside, it is not the cause of but merely the occasion for his later adventures; when he is translated into a baron for a day, and when he is supposedly condemned to death for false impersonation, he does not acquire new qualities of mind but reveals unsuspected and latent ones. Where we might expect a progressive and dialectical interaction between character and events, a mutual moulding and determining, we are invited instead to attend to a succession of encounters whereby character is disclosed and incident precipitated. For all their theatrical effectiveness, the comedies are thus in one sense less dramatic than *novellistisch*, that is to say that they exploit little of the extra range and depth that drama is capable of and instead adopt the economical, almost laconic style that is the essence of the Old Italian *novella*. Indeed it is arguable that only by operating within the brevity and lucidity of this tradition can one successfully pile up incident beyond ordinary expectation to the extent Holberg does and at the same time keep it exempt from confusion. These dramas have much more in common with Boccaccio than might be supposed from their dialogue form.

Yet whatever generalizations one might venture, there is always *Erasmus Montanus* to make one cast about for reservations. Generally in Holberg, it might be said we applaud the pricking of a balloon; the capers of his people are the means of inflation—peasant into baron, servant into master, lady's maid into Parisian dame—and the prick is not to make us wince but to deflate. But the complexity of inner growth in *Erasmus Montanus* seems to demand a different metaphor; and anyone who has observed the action of a hormone weed-killer, anyone who has pondered the grotesque and terrifying comedy of the plant falling victim to its own eagerness to absorb an excess of what in small doses contributes to its health until, bulging and straining, it collapses under the weight of its own grossness—anyone who has seen this must surely find there an appropriate image. The mind of the hero, the absurd young pedant returning home from University, is a rank growth running rife in the sour soil of Danish academic life; it is allowed and encouraged to proliferate, to feed on the opportunities for display; an excessive appetite for that which in itself is admirable—the chance to defend abstract truth against ignorant bigotry—causes it to become twisted and eccentric, until finally under the strain of its own bloated development it expires.

Holberg was a successful man. Many of his admirers have expressed surprise that, after amassing a modest fortune by shrewd investment in land, he should have accepted a barony in

1747 from the hands of Frederick V. How could it be, it was asked, that the author of a work like *Social Ambition*, that a man who had directed the sharpest satire against the folly of seeking social preferment, could so easily put aside his principles where his own person was concerned? But to ask this is to lose sight of something that currently unites his life and his authorship: that Holberg himself does with impunity what is the undoing of many of his created characters. He *is* Jean de France, he *is* Erasmus Montanus, but with a sense of practical living that saved him from folly. He was not only capable, he was sure of himself; in his youth he saw clearly his main objectives—

> Jeg skriver ene ej for at moralisere;
> For Folk ej ene, men og Sproget at polere

—to give not only moral guidance to the people but also polish to the language; nobody will deny his solid results in both. His acceptance of a title is surely an appropriate conclusion to a career that in all its aspects bore the signs of sane and practical and worldly achievement.

3

FROM HOLBERG TO WERGELAND

In the audience at the Christiania Theatre on the evening of Sunday, 28 January 1838, was a compact group of about thirty to forty people which included some of the capital's best known and most eminent citizens. They had been round the shops the day before to buy up all they could in the way of tin whistles and toy trumpets and the like; and a few hours before the performance began, they sent a note to the author of the piece that was to be performed which said: 'Perhaps your party may win this evening, but we will deliver you a resounding blow!' Inside the theatre they disposed themselves with care, and (according to a newspaper the next day) set up their headquarters in the stalls and put another detachment in one of the boxes; and then, as the performance progressed, they solemnly and deliberately gave it the bird. Their opponents responded from other points in the theatre with whatever came to hand—apples, paper balls, quids of tobacco and coins. Afterwards the aggressors could claim that in spite of their conspicuous bruises they had at least dealt their blow, for the performance was abandoned and the evening ended in complete disorder. But in no sense was it a famous victory.

The issues on this occasion lay thickly stratified; certainly they had little to do with the artistic merits of the work (called *The Campbells*) that was to have been performed. Uppermost lay those personal motives that gave the incident the appearance of being an attack on the reputation and standing of the author: Henrik Arnold Wergeland. At a deeper level were the factional interests, the promotion of and the opposition to those literary, cultural, social, political and national policies that had come to be associated with Wergeland's name. But below it all was a bed-rock of a thousand years of Norwegian history running from the age of national grandeur, through the long centuries of Norway's subservience to Denmark right up to the new age of political independence that had begun with the year 1814. In 1816 a book written by Nicolai Wergeland, the father of the poet, had appeared with the title *A True Account of Denmark's Political Crimes against the Kingdom of Norway from 955 to 1814.* In it the author claimed to adduce 'evidence enough that Norway, having suffered the insult of Denmark through the course of generations, had gained nothing and lost all . . . lost its kings, its freedom, its courts, its fleet, its flag, its language, its territories, its resources and its name in the political and literary world'. This is not the place to argue whether such accusations represent a balanced and objective picture of Norway's history; what is immediately relevant, however, is the realization that views of this kind and of this degree of bitterness were at the time widely held and loudly proclaimed. The country was naturally and rightly proud of its new constitution that had been drawn up and adopted at Eidsvoll on 17 May 1814; and indeed it was one of the most progressive in the world and an object of admiration and envy for the people of many less fortunate states. But those empty centuries of union with Denmark stood there as a constant humiliation to a people anxious to assert their pride in their country and their history; and of all the freedoms that Norway won for herself after the confused events of 1814, when after anxious months of political and military activity Norway was eventually declared to be 'a free, independent, indivisible and inalienable kingdom united with Sweden under one king', it was probably the freedom from domination by Copenhagen that appealed most strongly to popular sentiment. The notorious 'whistle concerto' of 1838 was a symptom of the social fever of these years, when Norway was defining her hopes and debating her cultural aspirations for the future.

However one may care to define what had been 'Norwegian' in the life and letters of the twin kingdoms of Denmark–Norway before 1814, there was certainly very little that did not in some way or other bear the stamp of Copenhagen—the seat of Government, the centre of culture, and the only university in the kingdom. Admittedly in the seventeenth century there had been the work of Petter Dass which was almost wholly free from Danish influence; living in the far north of Norway, he had written verses that lived on the lips of those who knew them, verses that needed no assistance from the printer's art in order to survive; his *Trumpet of the North Land* (*Nordlands Trompet*, begun 1678 and completed some time after 1692, first printed 1739), a simple and moving account of the life and landscape of northern Norway and of the duties and dangers of a parson's life there, was not printed until its author had been dead thirty years. Ludvig Holberg, although born in Bergen and in many ways demonstrably Norwegian, nevertheless lived and worked and wrote for the greater part of his life in Copenhagen.

Not quite twenty years after Holberg's death 'The Norwegian Society' (Det norske Selskap) was established in 1772 in Copenhagen; it owed its establishment to the initiative of a group of Norwegians living there, acting in a flush of national pride after one of their number, Nordahl Brun, had won a literary competition with the tragedy *Zarine* (1772). Its aims were convivial, patriotic and literary, probably for most members in that order of importance although literary history tends to reverse the order. To dismiss it, as one of Crown Prince Frederick's advisers contemptuously did, as 'a certain drinking club', is no doubt going too far, even though a well-known painting showing one of its evening meetings at Madame Juel's coffee house had as its most conspicuous object a punch bowl. It seems clear, however, that the cohesive force that held the Society together for forty years (though with a considerable turn-over in membership) was in the first place national and patriotic sentiment. True, it offered prizes for literary competition, and it had an official literary policy which was in general terms to promote the chaste and disciplined style of French classical poetry and eschew the more tempestuous and emotional style of England and Germany; moreover it sustained a lively feud with the subsequently formed (and significantly named) 'Danish Literary Society'. Yet whatever poetic as distinct from patriotic zeal there was belonged rather to a few individuals—it is reckoned that less than one-tenth of the members had any literary pretensions—and the works they produced were rather the result of the generally stimulating intellectual atmosphere of Copenhagen than of any corporate inspiration. When Nordahl Brun himself returned to Norway (eventually to become Bishop of Bergen), he wrote in 1788 to one of his friends in the Society: 'I made up my mind to sing, but at once I realized how greatly the things that daily surround us affect our souls. Here all we see are business affairs; here all we hear about are rates of exchange, stocks, freights, dried cod and stockfish.'

Of its members, it was not the earnest, ambitious Nordahl Brun, nor the intellectual Claus Fasting who made it immortal, but the talented yet feckless Johan Herman Wessel, the Society's licensed jester and of all its members the one who was probably least concerned about the objects that it officially endeavoured to promote—making up for this by his interest in its less official and more alcoholic proceedings. By reducing to brilliant absurdity what his colleagues took seriously, he produced in 1772 the one work that by its purely literary achievement—excluding, that is, Brun's poem 'For Norway, the warrior's birthland', which in spite of its banality had a patriotic success—makes the 'Norwegian Society' an item worthy of more than the historian's interest: the uproariously funny tragi-comedy *Love Without Stockings* (*Kierlighed uden strømper*). Strangely, considering the professed allegiances of their respective authors, it is a kind of dramatic counterpart to Lessing's *Hamburgische Dramaturgie* of five years earlier, a rapier attack on what Lessing had called 'the French scribblers': where Lessing slashes at the clumsy and unimaginative handling of the dramatic unities, Wessel flicks woundingly with his dramatic wit: everything in this deliberately most transparent and mechanical of plots occurs on the one day and in the one room, thanks to the most excruciating of contrivances. It has all the apparatus beloved by the imitators of French classical tragedy, the high-flown monologues, the confidantes, the spiritual conflict, and ends with a succession of suicides, the last of which are undertaken just to keep the others company; the prophetic dream that turns the crank of the plot is eventually discovered to be not the ineluctable voice of Fate but the result of the heroine's over-indulgence in peas, pork and herring. In its mock-heroism, it alone of the products of the Society successfully maintains the traditions of Holberg in the later years of the century.

Once rid of Copenhagen's domination, however, Norway in the years that followed 1814 saw her mission as that of building her future upon her own native traditions and of developing an indigenous culture. It was to this that her whole public life and cultural endeavour were geared. The new epoch began, however, at a time of economic crisis and cultural impoverishment, and any thoughts of spectacular achievement were frustrated by the lack of public money; private purses were also too light to allow individuals much thought to anything but the sterner business of living. The University of Christiania, founded in 1811, had not yet had time to establish itself properly as a force in the intellectual life of the nation; in the capital itself there was in the early years disappointingly little to nourish the mind or the spirit, and even bookshops were rare. By the 1830s, things had, it is true, improved in many ways: the worst of the economic privations were past, the first generation of scholars had made their reputations at the University, and a public theatre was established in Christiania in 1827—although it is perhaps significant as an index of the difficulties facing an ambitious country that the actors were Danish, and the director a Swede.

In this country of just over a million inhabitants, the three towns of Trondheim, Bergen and Christiania were not so dissimilar in the size of their population, each having something over 20,000 inhabitants; but there is no doubt that the capital city of Christiania had its own special character. The unexpected thing is that this special character derived not so much from the fact of its being the royal residence, nor even from its being the seat of government, but because it was the students' city. 'There is no country where youth is less neglected, and more listened to, than it is in Norway', wrote R. G. Latham, Fellow of King's

College, Cambridge, after a visit there in the summer of 1833; and he went on: 'A very large proportion of the press is entirely the contribution of the students of the University.' One of the consequences of the years of economic depression had been to accelerate the transfer of power within the country from the older merchant families to the ranks of the officials, that is to those professional classes who now studied at their own national university instead of at Copenhagen as their predecessors had done; and in the circumstances, with a city the size of Christiania, it was not surprising that the students were continuously active, both individually and corporately. It was a vigorous and rumbustious society, in which patriotism served as an excuse for almost any kind of extravagance; it was addicted to appeals and student rhetoric and heated argument, it was given to proclamation rather than analysis, it ranked ardour above logic, and was inclined to admire the energetic before the contemplative mind. The city itself was scarcely big enough to sustain impersonal discussion of matters of public concern; ideas, policies, doctrines were associated with individuals; persons and personalities counted. Arguments became contests in shouting down your opponent, the coarse witticism took the place of elegant wit, and truculent youth had most of the advantages.

But it seems that youth needs the challenge of age, or at least requires some sort of accepted convention or settled tradition to set itself against; and that, in Norwegian literature at least, was just what was lacking. The new literature could not help but be a kind of deliberate, and even in part planned, creation out of nothing. It was subject to strains not unlike those that accompany the making of a New Town in our own day, particularly those that go with the lack of any middle-aged or elderly elements, things which to youth seem to act only as a drag on its enthusiasms but which in some degree exert a beneficial stabilizing influence. In the case of Norway in these years, however, there was an additional complicating factor: here was a country that in one sense was a new nation but in another sense was an ancient kingdom; and alongside the political immaturity went a deep-rooted tradition of nationhood. This is a factor that needs to be continuously borne in mind when assessing the achievement of these young Norwegian writers. Their nationalism, which took the familiar and unexceptionable forms of seeking to be separate and distinct in their language and culture and institutions and of desiring to win acknowledgement from the rest of the world, was of ancient ancestry. And if on occasion they were perhaps a shade too eager to assume a close identity between the more general virtues of truth and liberty and beauty on the one hand and the narrower abstractions of Norwegiandom and Norwegianization on the other, one makes sympathetic allowance. This was the new spirit of which Wergeland was the embodiment; it was through his writings that it found its most genial expression, and through his example that the urgency and impatience and enthusiasm and excess were translated into deed.

It is doubtful whether Wergeland or any of those associated with him had any very clear image of what it was they so ardently sought and to which they paid such eager homage—except they were agreed it went with a strong Danophobia. 'Wergeland . . . is not only not for the Danes,' wrote Latham who had known him personally, 'but bitterly against them. His dislike of them amounts to a prejudice, an antipathy, a passion.' He felt a great contempt for this easy-going people to whom the cry of 'liberty' seemed to mean so little; the words 'Dane' and 'Danish' became for him terms of contemptuous abuse; he considered the Danish language—'that easy-going, soft, syrup-like, sherbet-like Danish', he said—to be something that in its own subtle way undermined the independence and the innate nobility of the Norwegian people. In 1831 he was even moved to suggest that 'all Norwegians returning home from Copenhagen should be subjected to fourteen days quarantine, especially when it comes to moral and aesthetic matters.' In terms of daily conduct, Wergeland's ideals took the form of careless disdain for fine manners and elegant ways, a conspicuous indifference to social convention, and a preference for whatever was homespun, all of these things being a kind of protest against what he felt to be the effete tradition of Danish manners. His father has told how he took courses in physical culture, how he would make a point of swimming in ice-filled rivers in late autumn, how he demanded meals of bear-flesh and horse-flesh, how he even invited his friends to share his meals of roast puppy and roast snake. It was an aggressively simple and ostentatiously frugal mode of life he adopted, making a cult of hardiness. And so too, no doubt, Wergeland envisaged the new national literature of his homeland; just as Norway's rugged landscape contrasted with the gentler aspects of the Danish scene, and just as the more forcefully articulated Norwegian speech was different from the less vigorous sounds of spoken Danish, so, too, the poetry of Norway was to hold to its own proper idiom and bear witness to a hardier way of life. Not for nothing did Wergeland's supporters call themselves 'the Patriots'.

It was mainly this aspect of things that drew the protests of 'the Intelligentsia', as they liked to call themselves—their opponents called them 'the Danophiles'. They deplored the 'rawness' and crudity of it all; they disapproved not only of the way in which Wergeland personally conducted himself in public but also of the ostentatious primitivism in the conduct of these self-styled 'patriots' who gave him support and encouragement. Claiming that they were as genuinely Norwegian as any of their neighbours, they nevertheless made no secret of their reluctance to jettison everything Danish; they insisted that culture was indivisible and urged that whatever was valuable in the Danish tradition should be retained and assimilated. The acknowledged spokesman of this group was Johan Sebastian Welhaven, whose initial protest in verse—the poem 'To Henrik Wergeland' ('Til Henrik Wergeland', 1830)—marked the opening of a long and bitter personal feud between the two men. Wergeland's reaction was to direct a stream of epigrams against the 'Danophile' professional men and public officials. The exchanges soon became more personal and more scurrilous, and by the end of 1831 the feud had acquired a national notoriety. In 1832 Welhaven published his essay *Henrik Wergeland's Poetic Art* (*Henrik Wergelands Digtekunst og Polemik ved Aktstykker oplyste*), which was a coldly reasoned and carefully documented critical assault on his opponent's style and literary creed; and two years later there appeared under Welhaven's name a collection of some seventy-five polished and yet rather prim sonnets entitled *Norway's Dawn* (*Norges Dæmring*, 1834), in which Wergeland is never explicitly attacked by name but where the polemic intent is plain; a number of other popular beliefs and views were subjected to a rather devastating scrutiny in these sonnets, and many of the shafts must have gone home for the book provoked a tremendous popular reaction against its author; for a time, Welhaven was one of the most unpopular men in the country. Meanwhile Wergeland had sustained his attack by epigram and farce; his father had also come to his support, the first time in 1833 with a skilfully argued defence of his son's personality and work entitled *A Proper Judgement of Henrik Wergeland's Poetry and Character* (*Retfærdig Bedømmelse af Henrik Wergelands Poesie og Karakteer*); and in 1835 he published a much more indignant rejoinder called *Defence of the Norwegian People and a Detailed Criticism of the Infamous Publication 'Norway's Dawn'* (*Forsvar for det Norske Folk og udførlig Kritik over det berygtede Skrift 'Norges Dæmring'*). He also exhorted everybody to make a ceremonial bonfire of Welhaven's book at the next Independence Day celebrations, a thing which actually occurred at one or two places.

Thus by the mid-1830s the conflicting views and attitudes and policies which had been gathering force ever since 1814 were, if not wholly clarified, then at least personified, and had moreover been brought to a pitch of bitterness where it was almost intolerable that things should remain unresolved much longer. Welhaven was the object of much popular dislike, but nevertheless stood reasonably well with the authorities; he had conducted his case with skill and deftness but was out of sympathy with the general spirit of national aspiration. Wergeland, on the other hand, roused enormous popular enthusiasm; and for all his exhibitionism and lack of restraint, he was attuned to something deep in the national consciousness. This was the feud that eventually reached its climax in the 'whistle concerto' of 1838; it was a clash of personality and attitude that gave the first real impetus to Norwegian literature of modern times, and helped to make of literature and literary debate an instrument for the shaping of national destiny.

Of the feud itself, one thing remains to be said: that however much one may be inclined to sympathize with the protests of Welhaven and his friends against the cruder excesses of 'the Patriots', one must nevertheless indict Norway's 'Intelligentsia' on one serious count—that of failing to appreciate beneath the apparent surface crudity of Wergeland's poetry those elements of genuine greatness that have rightly made his name immortal. They failed to understand the primeval force that surges through his poetry and which (one must in honesty admit) was on occasion just as liable to drive his work down to utter bathos as it was at other times to carry it up to sublime heights. Although the 'Danophiles' may have won many a tactical battle, yet it was Wergeland who won and retained the affection of his people, and he who by his devotion to his ideals and by his unquenchable courage in the face of the blows dealt him by fate nevertheless endured.

∗ 4 ∗

HENRIK WERGELAND

So long as the arrangement was kept to themselves, and the document destroyed after it had served its purpose, Henrik Wergeland had no objection to providing a contemporary critic with a few helpful notes about himself. This was in 1842, when he was thirty-four years old.

Born in Christiansand 17 June 1808, of parents Curate Nicolai W. and Dorothea Thaulow.... Wergeland is the name of a farm in Evindvig in Outer Sogn, whence my grandfather who was parish clerk moved to Bergen. It is still in the possession of the family, which is well-known for the tallness of its members and for the fact that they tend to live long. . . . In 1817 my father was transferred to Eidsvoll as Rector, whereupon his son came to receive his education at Major-General Aubert's establishment, and then attended the Cathedral School in Christiania 1819–1825. Aubert gave him a spartan training, as he did also his own children, and that has perhaps contributed to the health and strength W. enjoys, even though by nature his constitution is more than usually strong. As early as 1821, in the second form at school, he began to write for *Morgenbladet*, which at that time was more interested in aesthetic things. In 1825 he took his school leaving examination with 'laud'; by the spring of 1829, he had taken his Second Examination and his theological exams with 'haud'. By that time he had already published *Creation, Man and Messiah, The Death of Sinclair*, a volume of poems and a number of farces under the pseudonym of Siful Sifadda. His first independently published work, the farce *Ah!*, appeared under that name in 1826.[1] Led a fairly gay life, and has hardly any special learning in theology; yet in his preaching the public found much favour. With the exception of a journey to France and England in 1831 and a tour round Norway in 1832 and frequent visits to Christiania, he lived at his father's until the autumn of 1834, when he enrolled as a

[1] Actually 1827.

student of medicine. He did not make any headway with the Department of Church Affairs, despite the fact that the King admired him, and despite his having published a series of educational pamphlets and having used his popularity to found a number of small public libraries. This is confirmed also by the readiness with which he offered his services for the promotion of adult education, and also by his acting as a speaker at Independence Day celebrations, and not least by the open-air speech he held before an enormous crowd and before the Storting on 17 May 1833 on the occasion of the unveiling of the monument to the late Minister of State, Christian Krohg. His work as an author can be divided into the following categories:

1. Purely poetic: *Creation, Man and Messiah* [*Skabelsen, Mennesket og Messias*, 1830]; two volumes of poems [*Poems: First Cycle (Digte: Første Ring*, 1829) and *Poems: Second Cycle (Digte: Anden Ring*, 1833)]; the tragedies *The Death of Sinclair* [*Sinclars Død*, 1828] and *The Child Murderess* [*Barnemordersken*, 1835]; the dramas *Opium* [written 1828, published 1831] and *The Indian Cholera* [*Den indiske Cholera*, 1835] along with *The Cottage* [*Hytten*, 1838], the play *The Campbells* [*Campbellerne*, 1838] with two prologues, as well as two unpublished ditto[1] and a quantity of lesser, scattered verse. Separately published are the poems *Cæsaris* [1833], *The Blue Sea* [*Blaamyra*, 1832], *The Spaniard* [*Spaniolen*, 1833], *Jan van Huysum's Flower Piece* [*Jan van Huysums Blomsterstykke*, 1840], *The Swallow* [*Svalen*, 1841], and the two small collections or cycles *The Dulcimer* [*Langeleiken*, 1842] (poems in dialect), and *The Jew* [*Jøden*, 1842].

2. Satirical: the farces *Ah!* [1827], *Irreparabile tempus* [1828], *Harlequin virtuos* [1830], *Fantasies* [*Phantasmer*, 1829], *There is no arguing for tastes* [*Om Smag og Behag man ikke disputere*, 1832], *The Parrot* [*Papegøien*, 1835] with an attached polemic piece called *The Commentary*, *Traveller to Stockholm* nos. 1 and 2 [*Stockholmsfareren*, 1837], *Norway in 1800 and 1836* [*Norge i 1800 og 1836*], *The Last Wise Men* [*De sidste Kloge*, 1835], *The Pretzel* [*Kringla*, 1839], *English Salt* [*Engelsk Salt*, 1841], *Vinæger's Mountain Adventure* [*Vinægers Fjeldeventyr*, 1841], *The Bullfinch* [*Dompapen*, 1840], '*The World Belongs to us Lawyers*' ['*Verden tilhører Os Jurister!*', 1840]. With these belong also his *Sifuliners* [1832], i.e. epigrams directed against Welhaven, together with a lot of other scattered things.

3. Philanthropic (sit venia!): *For the General Public*, nos. 1 to 6 [*For Almuen*, 1830 ff.], *A Reader for the Public* [*Læsebog*, 1830], *The*

---

[1] *Sea Cadets ashore (Søkadetterne iland)*, written (?)1839, publ. 1848; and *The Venetians (Venetianerne)*, perf. 1841, publ. 1843.

Norwegian's Catechism [*Normandens Katechisme*, 1832], *Folksongs* [*Folkeviser*, 1832], *Veslebrun's Tale* [*Tale* . . . , 1833] (on our duties towards animals), *Contribution to the Jewish Affair* [*Indlæg i Jødesagen*, 1841], the periodical *For the Working Classes* [*For Arbeidsklassen*, 1839 ff.], three years.

4. Historical: *Norway's History*, in two parts [*Norges Historie*, 1834], *The History of Carl Johan after his Election in Sweden* [*Kong Carl Johans Historie*, 1837], *The History of Norway's Constitution* [*Norges Konstitutions Historie*, 1841 ff.]. . . .

5. Speeches: 'At Krohg's Monument', 'To the memory of our forefathers', speeches on Independence Days, 'The Speech *I* would give at the Akershus Electoral Meeting', a collection of sermons . . .

Apart from this there are a number of political and satirical articles in prose and verse in different papers, especially *Morgenbladet*. Acted 1835–37 as editor of the *Citizen*. . . . Was appointed amenuensis at the University Library 1836, whereupon he abandoned medicine, but prejudiced himself with the Government and the King by his politics. Regained the latter's favour by his poem 'The King's Arrival' in December 1838, so that he had hopes of a curateship, which he was aiming at because he had become engaged to a girl without means of her own. But one evening he was caught with the Officer of the King's Guard along with a party of rather merry people who had brought along some punch and a guitar. Proceedings were taken against the officer, and the curacy went up in smoke. The King then awarded him a couple of hundred *daler* for two years, with the possibility of more, which W. accepted for use in adult education work. It was then that he published the paper *For the Working Classes*. Later, His Majesty granted him 300 *Speciedaler* for a further two years and in the autumn of 1840 had him appointed Director of the State Archives. He married in the spring of 1839 and has built himself a little villa at a nice spot near Christiania, called The Grotto, because the house really does stand over a grotto in the rock. His onetime friends forgot that W. had always been an enthusiastic supporter of Carl Johan, and treated him dreadfully as a renegade, for which in none of his recent writings is there a single trace of evidence.

Everything about Wergeland was prodigious, not excluding his faults. And in admitting this, it is prudent also to distinguish three different aspects of him which, whilst they cannot always be kept entirely separate, nevertheless should not be wantonly confused: one is the part he played in national life as an agent or representative of urgent political forces; another is his individual example and the impact of his personality upon his fellows, which can be traced from his somewhat equivocal beginnings through years of renunciation to his final and quietly magnificent display of personal courage; and a third is his stature as a formal artist.

It is not easy to know how best to define his early life: as an education in freedom; as an indoctrination in liberalism; or as a training in precociousness. What we do know is that before the boy was a year old, his father had brought out what he referred to as the *Henricopædia*, a handbook for parents in which he outlined the liberal principles he believed ought to govern the upbringing of children. The young Wergeland learnt the art of not allowing modesty or diffidence to hamper him; he was taught to meet life as a challenge, in which confidence and courage were the things that counted; and he was given a sense of dedication. Whatever else the consequences, it resulted in his coming to his adult mission equipped with a superb outward self-assurance. It was the sheer uninhibited force of his personality, and his gift of exacting from his supporters an immediate loyalty, rather than any great skill in the formulation of ideas and policies, that made of him, even as a young man, one of the most influential forces in the life of Norway.

Yet it was a spiteful game that Fate played with him, endowing him with rare gifts and encouraging him with dreams of high endeavour and yet incessantly imposing on him and his wrestle with life's problems an inauthentic solution, smiling sweetly to his face only to turn away with a snigger. He was strident in his Norwegian pride, yet felt very keenly the frustration of belonging to a small nation tucked away in the corner of the world, with a language (as he put it) 'that stretches no further from its corner than the breath from its lips'; in 1829 he seriously thought of writing in German that he might make himself more widely known, and at another time he pondered leaving Norway and trying to make his career in England. He was a giant of a fellow, strong and hardy (and rather proud of it, as his autobiographical notes show), yet unexpectedly short-sighted and rather comically bespectacled. He hungered for friendship and intimacy, yet much of his life was a career in personal disappointment and growing isolation. He yearned for and eloquently expressed his love of woman, yet seemed to frighten the girls away—whilst still a young man he had four separate and ardent proposals of marriage rejected, and for long years was compelled to devote himself to a bloodless abstraction of ideal Womanhood he called 'Stella'. After one jilting, he sought an ostentatious death by flinging himself off the high ramp of a barn, only to land (possibly as a result of his shortsightedness) literally in clover, unharmed. (And yet it belongs equally to the account that he was ready to tell this story against himself, and indeed tell it on his death-bed.) He was filled with a sense of the heroic; he shaped his personality to conform to the traditional Norse virtues, and ordered his behaviour as though it were his duty to prove himself in combat as his forefathers had done, to assert his leadership and display a proper aggressiveness; yet there was withal, perhaps in his own temperament or else in the climate of the age, something inimical to such traditional expressions of the heroic; no truthful picture of Wergeland dare omit reference to those occasions when, urged on towards some heroic deed, he found himself embroiled in some situation distressingly unheroic, such as when his eagerness to seek valorous combat betrayed him into what was nothing more than a drunken brawl. How appropriately symbolic it now seems that, once when his motives in defending his friend's good name were high but where the reality of the occasion was merely sordid, he should have cast into his opponent's face not the gauntlet of chivalry but a pig's ear:

I got home last night [he wrote to a friend on 23 January 1827] after an 'Aquavit' binge and a hell of a fight between Larsen the bailiff and me. My ears are full of blood. It happened when he called Lerche a filthy pig, whereupon I cut one of the ears off a pickled boar's head and threw it in his face; it came back, so then I gave him a box on the ears; then a couple back from the glazier, so I pulled the sheriff over and hit Larsen in the eye. Then I found myself on the floor and was overpowered.—When I got up I hit him again, and got the worst of it again; I hit him again, and again I took a beating, but mainly because I was anxious about my spectacles that were lying on the floor, and because he grabbed my testicles.

He leapt to the support of the underprivileged, championed the oppressed with bold words, but when he denounced a grasping, Danish-born landlord as 'a criminal against the state and against humanity', Wergeland found himself challenged not to mortal combat but instead to defend himself in the courts, where a seemingly endless lawsuit dragged on numbingly for over twelve years and ultimately impoverished him.

Behaviour that made a popular hero of him in certain circles stamped him with the authorities as an irresponsible trouble-maker, headstrong and immoderate. He was fond of his liquor, but had no great head for it, and there were many escapades that embarrassed the authorities and steadily reduced his chances of the living he repeatedly applied for. In 1835 he became the father of an illegitimate child by a servant girl in the employment of the dean; in 1837 he was arrested for a disturbance in the public street; of the episode involving the King's Guard he has himself spoken. There can be little doubt he was a sore trial even to many who wished him well, and among his own supporters there were some who now and then found him insufferable, as the evidence of one of them clearly shows: 'His presence was not an occasion for unmixed pleasure. We preferred having him at a distance, even though he possessed the enthralling power of genius; he always wanted to be top dog in the company, and held speech after speech of which we ordinary mortals did not understand a word but at the end of which we clapped and shouted "Hurrah!" with all our might.' Even his father admitted that he had 'temperamental failings discomfiting for his friends, infuriating to his enemies, and damaging to himself'.

After 1838, however, a change came over Wergeland's life, as also over his work. (Actually Wergeland himself put the change somewhat earlier, in 1834; and in the covering letter he sent with the brief autobiographical notes, he admitted that as a younger man he had lacked the faculty of self-criticism, but that in more recent years he had been a stern judge of his own actions.) He had succeeded in making a little money out of *The Campbells*; he now had an appointment, which to begin with had only been temporary, at the University Library; and he had also proposed marriage and been accepted. In March 1839 he agreed, in spite of his anti-royalist views, to accept a grant from the Crown, provided that he might use it for adult educational work and nothing else; but his motives were misinterpreted in a number of quarters, so that he found himself estranged from many of those who had been his staunchest friends, who now made no secret of their feeling that Wergeland had betrayed both them and the cause. In November 1840 Wergeland was made State Archivist, and at the same time Welhaven was appointed to a Lectureship in Philosophy at the University. Once again the news was received with much adverse public criticism and with private hostility, and Wergeland suffered grievously under the accusation that he had ceased to be a man of the people and had gone over to become a King's man. He began to live a much more reserved kind of life; a greater element of restraint showed itself in his writing, and a greater sense of tolerance in his opinions— it was at this time that he espoused the Jewish cause, attacking the paragraph in the Constitution that forbade them entry into the country; he wrote his *Contribution to the Jewish Affair*, his poem cycle *The Jew*, and later *The Jewess* (*Jødinden*, 1844).

It was then Fate dealt what seemed to be the last sardonic blow. This man who was so proud of his robust constitution, whose family was (as he had pointed out) so well-known for the longevity of its members, died at the age of thirty-seven of a chill:

It was the old walls of Akershus that brought me to this [he wrote from his sickbed in November, 1844]. They stoked up the stoves too much for me during the last few days of April, when we had some sunny weather, and I gave orders that they could at least stop lighting the stove in my room. I arrive at the office warm, throw off my jacket and sit down at my desk in my shirtsleeves without thinking that the stove was not on. After about an hour I felt such shivers down my back that I had to go home, and I have now been lying here since 2 May. So it is my own fault. After pneumonia there followed tuberculosis of the lung.

He died, after fifteen months of illness and pain, on 12 July 1845. But that was not in fact the final paradox: that came when Wergeland, after what had very largely been a career of cumulative frustration in his aggressive and assertive assaults on life, now by his simple, quiet and resigned courage in the face of inexorably approaching death won an undying victory in defeat. He went on writing with incredible spirit to the last, completing his long narrative poem *The English Pilot* (*Den engelske Lods*, 1844), completely revising his *Creation, Man and Messiah* and re-publishing it as *Man* (*Mennesket*, 1845), and compiling his deceptively light-hearted autobiographical sketches *Hazelnuts* (*Hassel-Nødder*, 1845). His example impressed the whole nation, and shamed those of his friends who had turned against him. His funeral procession was a demonstration of popular affection that has gone down in history.

His reputation among his friends as the Byron of Norway was one that Latham could not permit himself to endorse:

He eschewed neckcloths, and delighted not in watery potations. No likeness beyond this, and the fact of both being poets, was discoverable. When I saw him for the first time, he recalled to my mind the likenesses I had seen of Burns; except that he was bigger by some four inches, and heavier by some three stone. Six feet three without his shoes is a good bard-like stature. . . . For my own part, I make him out to have more of the author of the Corn Law Rhymes in him, than he has of anyone else. If I delighted in coining compounds after the manner of those who talk of Cromwell-Grandison's, and Cobbett-Burke's I should call him an Elliott-Ossian.

Latham's coinage still retains some of its currency. There was in Elliott much that Wergeland would surely have approved of— the fervour of the political convictions, the earnest passion of the verses, and the quality that Carlyle once defined by further cross-reference as the 'slight bravura touch of the fair youthful Hemans'. And as for Ossian, Wergeland himself would not only have rejoiced in the comparison but in one way positively invited it. By choosing for his farces and for a number of the other slighter pieces the pseudonym 'Siful Sifadda', Wergeland re-

called the passage in Ossian's 'Fingal' where Cuthullin rides out
to do heroic battle with Swaran, in a car of war drawn by two
snorting horses, one of them called Dusronnel and the other the
'high-maned, broad-breasted, proud, wide-leaping, strong steed
of the hill', Sulin Sifadda. So it was, heroically and in double
harness, that Wergeland rode his genius like a chieftain of old
rolling in search of the foes of his land, striking the bossy shield
so that the hills and rocks of Norway resounded; and when he
lashed out at his opponents with epigram and farce, it was again
as in Ossian that 'Sifadda bathed his hoof in blood'.

Two of his qualities as a writer are, however, not in question:
he was prolific, and he was versatile. He seemed, especially in his
earlier years, to be able to produce with all the prodigal fecundity
of Nature herself, giving his work the appearance not of a carefully cultivated garden (as was the case with Welhaven) but all
the abandoned luxuriance of a trackless landscape. Nor was there
anything choosy about his talent for words; he was ready to turn
his pen to anything, and did; and time seemed to present no
problem. A great deal of his energy went into the adult education
movement and into schemes for establishing public lending
libraries; and he was just as ready to sit down and compose
specimen bye-laws for these things as he was to write poetry.
A consistently representative edition of his works would therefore have to include many things of little intrinsic and negligible
literary value, whatever their historical or biographical significance: educational pamphlets, popular articles, speeches, patriotic
songs, polemic pieces and other fugitive products. What gives
these things their importance is what one might call their high
co-efficient of betrayal; they reveal much, they constitute an
involuntary autobiography, reflecting clearly and sometimes
mercilessly something of the mind that produced them.

A selection of his writings made on different lines—one that
does not set out to *exemplify* it but to select from it, taking only
what is excellent and suppressing what is mediocre or (as it sometimes is) catastrophic—such a selection yields a body of work of
strangely disturbing, uniquely impressive and in part sheerly
breath-taking quality. One turns above all to the lyric poems, and

to what is best in them. The change that is wrought on Wergeland by such an operation can perhaps most easily be appreciated by noting what happens to *The English Pilot* after a skilful editor has done his work. In this long poem, all that concerns the story —a tale of degenerate lords and virtuous commons, of true love thwarted by aristocratic villainy—is a scream; it reminds one of nothing so much as a bad imitation of Captain Marryat (whose translated works, incidentally, flooded the Danish and Norwegian book market after 1835, and whom Wergeland seems to have read avidly); but this story links together scattered passages of matchless lyric beauty that stand supreme in Norwegian literature, passages which shine with enhanced brilliance when stripped of their contextual dross. And thus it is also generally with Wergeland's larger scale work; as Latham very acutely puts it: 'Their great merit is the abundance of the grand essential, imagination. Their chief defect is the absence of a restraining judgement. It may be doubted whether Wergeland ever rejected an idea.' Possibly because he suspected his own weakness in self-criticism, he often invited his father to offer advice about his compositions; but many are ready to believe that that worthy man, whilst saving his son from a good many blunders, nevertheless ironed out too many of the wrong things. Wergeland's genius seemed to be of the kind that demanded at all costs to be kept going, dreading a stoppage and happy to work away on any material that it might thus keep itself bright and serviceable. There can surely be few poets of such undoubted greatness who have written (or at least published) so much bad poetry; there is plenty to justify Gosse's remark that Wergeland combined 'the characteristics of a divine poet and a stump orator'. The consequence is that, collected, his works are monstrous; anthologized, they are a miracle.

From the start, his poetry was marked by a richly luxuriant and startlingly audacious imagery, being so obviously the work of one who was exposed to a welter of impressions, of which the very logic of their setting down is the logic not so much of orderly progression as of run-away association. His work gives the impression of being charged with a desperate anxiety to record

things before they were lost; the concentration has been on getting them down, ignoring for the time being the contorted word
order, the frequent latinisms and the zealous use of parenthesis;
the final ordering, they seem to say, can wait. Their spontaneity
is their most obvious and their most admirable quality. The central
feature of these early poems is 'Stella'. This was, initially and in
part, a code name for the girl currently in favour, but its fuller
meaning was something that Wergeland ceaselessly and energeti-
cally extended and expanded until it stood in some contexts for
the spiritual and predestined bride who was to complement and
bring to a new and fully realized unity Wergeland's own self, in
other settings for some idealized and on the whole denatured
concept of Womanhood, and eventually it became the symbol of
some irresistible cosmic power. In the introductory poem 'To
Stella' ('Til Stella'), she is the woman who remains remote in
this life but who will be united with him in passionate love after
death, just as they were once united also in some pre-existence;
'A Song-filled Summer Morning on Skreya' ('En sangfuld som-
mermorgen paa Skreya') distances Stella into dream, in which
the poet, knowing he is to be united with his Stella in after-life,
dreams of seeking heroic death in Greece in the fight for liberty;
he imagines the fusion of their spirits into one, sees the ethereal
thing gliding through the heavens 'like a two-necked swan'. And
in the last poem of this collection, it is related how the two souls
of the poet and his Stella journey through the realms of the stars,
seeing there the work of creation, and on to a celestial wedding;
there, in a state of complete spirituality and having cast off their
earthly bodies, Stella takes her place alongside the other women
who have inspired great poets, Petrarch's Laura, Tasso's
Leonora, Byron's loves. What gives these early poems their
idiosyncratic flavour is that they are at one and the same time
egocentric and centrifugal; all the poems have a personal origin,
all are balanced on a point of subjectivity, but as soon as Wergeland's inspiration begins to move, these poems 'fly off', their
imagery is projected out into the wideness of heaven, out among
the stars where spirits dwell and the work of creation goes on.
There is in all things a reflection of the cosmos, even in the eye

of his little rabbit—'one-eared, three-legged, violet-blue and fine'
—he sees the universe mirrored. Of Rilke it was said that he
progressed in his poetry from 'things' to 'angels', omitting the
human stage; in Wergeland it is not that the poems are deficient
in human values but rather that these things are suppressed. One
might almost risk saying 'repressed'. The concrete experience of
living becomes an abstract idea, the immediacy of life and its
challenges and frustrations and complexities is projected up to
breathlessly cosmic heights. So that although many of these
poems are love poems, it is noteworthy that to *possess* the loved
one (except in some rarified, abstract way) was a thought that
Wergeland at this time did not, or dared not, allow into his
poetry; all is cosmic. Wergeland's characteristic posture, according to contemporary reports, is one in which his head is thrown
back and his gaze heaven-turned—the posture that Vigeland's
statue in fact gives him. Equally one could imagine him with the
down-turned eye of simple humility, communing with the
smaller creatures of Nature he writes of with so much affection.
What it is difficult to imagine, however, is Wergeland holding a
level stare, seeing life steadily and dispassionately, permitting
himself a direct and unswerving scrutiny of his own kind.

Creation, Man and Messiah was a conscious attempt to out-
Milton Milton, being nearly 20,000 lines long and filling some
720 pages of print; although if any direct influence is to be sought
it is perhaps rather to Byron and his *Heaven and Earth* that one
should turn. It was a direct development out of the earlier poems,
and in the event it became (as Wergeland himself said in a letter
to Elise Wolff, his 'Stella' of the moment) both a love poem and
a gigantic commentary on the world and its emergence from
Chaos. Through the medium of an extremely characteristic
Wergelandian pattern of invention, it offers an exposition of its
author's view of the world and also of his convictions concerning
Man's relationship to Woman. Two themes, traceable already in
the earlier poems, are given fuller imaginative definition: the idea
that Man, faced with the dilemma of having been created with
an animal as well as a spiritual side to his nature, is everlastingly
concerned with the problem of reconciling them; and the notion

that love is not only a force in the individual's life but is also the power that turns the universe. *Creation, Man and Messiah* thus became an extended statement on the origins of Man's great dilemma, and an expression of the hope he may have that these two apparently discordant elements in him might be brought into harmony. One marvels at the sheer size of the thing, boggles at its dimensions and the range and sweep of invention. Yet one is reminded perhaps not so much of a 'broad canvas' as of a 'wide screen'; it is colossal, gigantic, super-special in the way of a biblical film epic; its script is, as it were, 'adapted' from the Bible, whereby for instance Rachel is shown as being in love with Jesus, and Jesus by the rejection of her love for the sake of his mission driving her to sin, until finally their souls are united in love after death; it exploits the familiar blend of the religious, the sadistic and the erotic, and is sustained throughout by a brash faith in itself and in its own brand of naïve spirituality. Fourteen years after its publication, Wergeland himself admitted its faults; he worked on his sick bed to revise it, and petitioned the Norwegian Academic Society for a grant to publish the greatly revised version, stating: 'The poem suffers from all the defects of youth, from a formless rapturousness and lack of restraint; but some people have found poetic qualities in it that ought not to be left lying as they do now in a heap of deformities and obscurities, but which ought in some better form to rescue for literature this quite considerable poem.'

One is impelled to seek some explanation of why Wergeland's poetry in these years puts the emphasis on telling of the spiritualized and etherealized side of things whilst seeming at the same time to be sustained by a much more earthy kind of eroticism that is there as a concealed fundament—only occasionally does one come across things that startle by their very unethereal sensuousness, like the line in the 'Stella' poem that claims: 'Each kiss was like eating a ham.' And the temptation is to ascribe this phenomenon, at least in part, to a deep-seated mistrust of himself and his own private motives at the more mundane levels of life, and a recognition of his own vulnerability there. In spite of his often rather forbidding self-assurance, he seems both to have

4

feared for what might happen, and feared rebuff. His need for love and human affection, sometimes so pathetically obvious, served very often only to proclaim to others his vulnerability at this point; and his very craving for sympathy and approval tended only to draw the attacks of those who were hostile to him. It would be altogether understandable if he tended to withdraw into his abstractions because it was harder to hurt him there. It belonged to his own personal tragedy that he was never in his younger years able to enter into any really intimate relationship with any other man or woman; and both the 'Stella' poems and *Creation, Man and Messiah* strike one as being both a product of and a kind of justification for this state of affairs. His affection was reserved rather for the sub-human and the super-human, for the lowly and the lofty, for birds and flowers and rabbits and for celestial spirits and invented abstractions. There is a parallel to this in the way Wergeland yearned for really close contact with life's actualities; any opportunity to give practical help to those less fortunate than himself he seized with a genuinely altruistic and yet strangely selfish gratitude; he wanted so desperately to lay hold on life, and his capacity for giving of himself was immense; yet he appeared tragically inhibited. Similarly also, he wanted more than anything else to be a poet of the people; he was ready to honour at all times the concept of Man's equality, but nobody knew better than he that in reality nobody was his equal; his mode of thinking was cast in too aristocratic a mould, and he invited comparison more than once between his own status and that of the eagle. The language and the style of his poetry was much too difficult and esoteric to live on the tongues of ordinary folk—with certain obvious and triumphant exceptions.

The very considerable change that came over his life in the mid-1830s reached a culmination in 1838, the year he fell in love with a kindly, homely, simple-hearted girl, Sofie Bekkevold, who accepted his proposal of marriage. 'Of course she has no education,' wrote Wergeland's sister Camilla, 'but makes up for it by a naturally good intelligence and a completely unpretentious nature. In addition there is something happy about her—I mean that kind of outward friendliness and warmth that our family is so completely lacking in. What I most admire in her is her genuine feeling, a natural tact which is most admirable in one of her situation and environment.' It was as though her gentle innocence were to provide the key element that had been lacking in Wergeland's life, the cohesive force that would bring the anarchy of his ways of living and feeling and writing into a more reposeful unity. 'Stella' was what he had put central to his life earlier, but it had become obvious that that centre could not hold; now, to Sofie, he could write in one of his poems: 'You, innocent bride, have reconciled my soul with the world, my blood with God . . .' Her trust in him, her glad surrender, was the long-delayed affirmation of something in him that had for years been denied.

His work bore an immediate imprint; and the poems he wrote in 1838 and which were collected under the title of *Poesies* (*Poesier*) are among the most accomplished things he ever wrote. They are love poems with a much more genuine ring, the air of pretence is gone; these new poems stand to his own earlier work in much the same way as, say, the love poems of the young Goethe stand to those of the young Schiller, simple and natural and unforced and with none of the hothouse luxuriance of a fostered passion. The imagery is less hectic, the constructions less contorted, the mood less cosmically intense, the sentiment more immediately personal. From now until his death, it is obvious he gave much greater care to the composition of his more serious pieces, working with a keener sense of the unity of things than he had hitherto, making his poetry technically more efficient in the sense that less of the tremendous input power was lost in merely overcoming the internal friction of the imagery. Here it is, in the exquisite *Jan van Huysum's Flower Piece*, in *The Jew* and *The Jewess*, in *The English Pilot*, but most of all in *Poesies*, that the real treasure of his genius is to be found.

✳ 5 ✳

HENRIK IBSEN

Along familiarity with Ibsen has still not entirely succeeded in erasing the memory of his first introduction to England. One approaches him still, in the theatre and in the armchair, with certain strong if not always precisely formulated expectations that have their source in the 'nineties; he is enmeshed in a web of association, he is part of a familiar local scene. In this one respect he resembles Baudelaire, of whom it has been rightly said that the task of dissociating what is permanent in his art from what is temporary is partly the problem of detaching him from the associations of those English writers who first admired him, and partly a question of distinguishing the man from his influence.

A simple mnemonic fixes the general chronological pattern of Ibsen's work: his first drama *Catilina* was published pseudonymously at the age of twenty-two in 1850, and the corrected proofs of his final work *When We Dead Awaken* were delivered to the printer in the last December days of 1899; so that the span of his creative life corresponds almost exactly with the second half of the nineteenth century. In his fifty years of authorship he wrote twenty-five plays, the thirteenth of which, the enormous and ponderous 'double' drama *Emperor and Galilean* (*Kejser og Galilæer*, 1873), stands there as a watershed to his life's work—with the later and more characteristically 'Ibsenite' plays standing on one side of it, and the earlier and less characteristically so on the other. The immediate outward sign of the change in his work at this time is the deliberate adoption of a realistic prose dialogue as his dramatic medium in place of metrical verse. Edmund Gosse felt that *Emperor and Galilean* might have gained by being written in verse, and wrote to Ibsen to tell him so; Ibsen's reply of 15 January 1874 is forthright in its rejection of this idea:

You think that my play should have been in verse and that it would have gained by this. On that point I must contradict you, for the play is—as you have noted—cast in a form as realistic as possible; it was the illusion of reality I wanted to produce. I wanted to evoke in the reader the impression that what he was reading really happened. If I had used verse, I would have run counter to my intentions and to the task I have set myself. . . . My new play is no tragedy in the old style; what I wanted to portray was people, and it was precisely for that reason that I did not allow them to speak with 'the tongues of angels'.

A considerable part of his earlier work had been written in verse. *Catilina* written in the winter months of 1848–49, and about which Ibsen later wrote that many of the things round which his later writings revolved—'the contradiction between ability and ambition, between what is willed and what is possible, that which is Man's and the individual's tragedy and comedy at one and the same time—appear here faintly indicated'; *The Warrior's Barrow* (*Kjæmpehøjen*) and *Midsummer Eve* (*Sankthansnatten*) from the years 1850 and 1852 respectively but not published until much later; much of *The Feast at Solhoug* (*Gildet paa Solhoug*, 1856), for which Ibsen's reading of Norwegian folk songs provided inspiration; parts of *Olaf Liljekrans*, a romantic drama in three acts, performed at Bergen in January 1857 but not printed until 1898; and *Love's Comedy* (*Kjærlighedens Komedie*, 1862), a drama which contemporary criticism found both immoral and unpoetic, and which Ibsen later regretted having published at that time in Norway, saying that 'both time and place were an unfortunate choice'.

Yet even at this early stage in his career, Ibsen seemed to show greater assurance in prose: *Lady Inger at Ostraat* (*Fru Inger til Østeraad*) first performed in Bergen in January 1855 and published in 1857 is perhaps not particularly remarkable; but *The Vikings at Helgeland* (*Hærmændene paa Helgeland*, 1858) was an accomplished piece of dramatic composition in which, inspired by his reading of *Volsungasaga*, Ibsen attempted with some measure of success to find a modern approximation to the strong and purposeful language of the sagas; and with *The Pretenders* (*Kongs-Emnerne*, 1864), a drama which contrasted the easy confidence of Haakon with the complex and introspective nature of Skule, he produced what is the profoundest of these early works.

The Pretenders, written in the summer months of 1863, was performed in January 1864 in Christiania with moderate success. But by this year Ibsen was if not embittered then at least a disappointed man. He had experienced financial difficulties, many of his plays had been met with indifference and even outright hostility. The Norwegian parliament had refused him the 'poet's pension' it had recently granted to Bjørnson. Ibsen left Norway in April 1864 and for the next twenty-seven years was resident abroad almost without interruption, in Italy and Germany.

Brand, first conceived as an epic poem and then re-written as a verse drama, was completed in the summer of 1865 at Ariccia near Rome and published the following year in Copenhagen; it was followed in 1867 by *Peer Gynt*. These two 'non-theatrical' plays complement each other: *Brand* takes as its hero a Kierke-gaardian figure, unbending, uncompromising, sternly dedicated to the principle of 'all or nothing'; *Peer Gynt* follows the fantastic career of a person wholly unprincipled, buoyant, yielding, and content to adopt as his motto 'To thine own self be—enough'; where the one is admirable but unlovable, the other is lovable but reprehensible; and yet both can justifiably be considered in part as portraits of the author. 'Brand is myself in my finest moments', Ibsen is reported to have said; whilst Bjørnson on the other hand later said: 'Not till *Peer Gynt* did Ibsen become himself; for Peer Gynt *was* him.' To the 1860s belongs also that other dramatic work which in part spoils the neat geometry of the mnemonic: *The League of Youth* (*De unges Forbund*), completed in Dresden in 1869 and which in style and influence anticipates to some extent the later plays.

It was in the last quarter of the century, in the second half of his creative life, that Ibsen produced with almost metronomic regularity the series of twelve plays by which he was in England most generally known. These were the years in which the realistic 'problem' plays of Ibsen and Bjørnson gave Norwegian literature its leading position among the literatures of Europe, plays which appealed to a generation only too ready to receive them as exercises in social criticism. Beginning with *Pillars of Society* (*Samfundets støtter*) in 1877, Ibsen continued with those works whose titles alone are redolent of the powder and shot of controversy: *A Doll's House* (*Et dukkehjem*, 1879), *Ghosts* (*Gengangere*, 1881), *An Enemy of the People* (*En folkefiende*, 1882), *The Wild Duck* (*Vildanden*, 1884), *Rosmersholm* (1886), *The Lady from the Sea* (*Fruen fra havet*, 1888), *Hedda Gabler* (1890), *The Master Builder* (*Bygmester Solness*, 1892), *Little Eyolf* (*Lille Eyolf*, 1894), *John Gabriel Borkman* (1896), and *When We Dead Awaken* (*Naar vi døde vaagner*, 1900).

It is clear from this chronicle that Ibsen arrived late in England, in the more public sense of arrival; and it is also noteworthy that England was much later than Germany with her welcome. In the 1870s no fewer than six of Ibsen's plays had been translated into German, and indeed two of them, *Brand* and *Pillars of Society*, each appeared in three different translations; this is as against one play (and a bit) in English, and none in French. By 1890 there were altogether twenty-seven different German translations, covering sixteen of the plays, plus also two separate translations of his poems; in England, there were seven translations of five of the plays; in France, two of the plays had been translated. Moreover it is recorded that as early as 1878, there were in one particular week in February five different companies in Berlin alone all performing *Pillars of Society*. In England, the first influential translations did not appear until 1888, when there was published (in the Camelot Series) a volume edited and introduced by Havelock Ellis and containing *Pillars of Society* and *Ghosts* (both translated by William Archer) and *An Enemy of Society* (translated by the daughter of Karl Marx, Mrs. Eleanor Marx-Aveling); in the following year 1889 *A Doll's House* was performed, in Archer's translation, at the Novelty Theatre, the first (shall one say) 'substantial' Ibsen production in England. By this year, however, Ibsen was over sixty years old and had been writing plays for nearly forty of them.

One should not conclude from this that Ibsen was entirely neglected in England before these events. There had been the efforts of Edmund Gosse, who in 1872 as a young man of twenty-two had been commissioned by the *Spectator* and *Fraser's Magazine* to visit Scandinavia and report on the state of the literature there; in one of his four short and unsigned articles that same year he described Ibsen as 'second to none of his contemporaries', and introduced him as a writer who was prevented from enjoying the European reputation he deserved only by 'the remoteness of his mother tongue'. A further article of his the following year in the *Fortnightly Review* succeeded in awakening rather more interest in Ibsen in certain circles; and in 1879 there appeared in volume form his *Studies in the Literature of Northern Europe* which marked the culmination of a decade's enthusiastic but often uncritical endeavour on Ibsen's behalf. Meanwhile translations of a kind had begun to appear; the first—a most unexpected choice—was of *Emperor and Galilean* by Catherine Ray in 1876; and in a book published the same year and bearing the title *Translations from the Norse* (thought to be by a certain A. Johnston) there appeared, along with a number of Ibsen's poems, the first Act of *Catilina* together with a summary of Acts Two and Three. The first ever London production of an Ibsen play was on 15 December 1880 at the Gaiety Theatre: a play called *Quicksands*, a much mutilated version of *Pillars of Society*, translated by William Archer. Of this performance a Danish theatrical critic reported to his Copenhagen paper that the audience gave the play an enthusiastic reception and called loudly for the author, a request which 'was readily met, without any reserve or trace of embarrassment, by Mr. Archer, the English translator'. *A Doll's House* also had a fitful life on the London stage about this time. It was first (and very eccentrically) translated under the title of *Nora* by a Dane in 1880, again under the same title in 1883 by Henrietta Frances Lord, and yet again in 1884 by Henry Arthur Jones and Henry Herman, whose version was performed on 3 March at the Prince's Theatre with the so-called German or 'happy' ending, under the title of *Breaking a Butterfly*. If this title seems by implication to show sympathy for Nora, there was to counterbalance it the selection the following year of the authentic version of the play—which as is well known ends with Nora leaving home and slamming the door on her husband and children—for a charity performance by an amateur group calling itself 'The Scribblers' Dramatic Society', the occasion being an appeal on behalf of the then National Society for the Prevention of Cruelty to Children.

So it was that often in rather unexpected ways Ibsen made progress in this country—one might also mention with affection the keen propaganda work of the Rev. Philip Wicksteed, who about this time made it his habit to take the texts of his sermons from the pages of *Peer Gynt*, and who in his enthusiasm for Ibsen had, at a Hampstead school, conducted classes through the Norwegian text of *The Vikings at Helgeland*. After the pioneering work of Gosse, however, it was William Archer who made the more solid contribution to Ibsen's English reputation. He had met Ibsen in the winter of 1881–82 in Rome, and he went on to devote himself to the translation, editing and arranging of Ibsen's works. The English collected edition began to appear in 1906; in spite of the hard things that are said, sometimes justifiably, about the quality of the translation, it stands as a praiseworthy achievement.

It was not until the year 1891 that the storm broke, a year in which there were five of Ibsen's plays produced in London, including *Rosmersholm*, *An Enemy of the People* and, of course, *Ghosts*. The violence of the press reaction is well known. Ibsenism was then under way and under fire.

The official histories of the original Ibsenite campaign rightly pay close attention to the generalship of Shaw. From our present standpoint in time, one can delight in the vigour of his *Quintessence of Ibsenism*, in the thrustful aggressiveness of his defence, in the brilliant intuition that informed him of the weaknesses in the opposition and his cruel probing of them; but many are now ready to admit that his brilliance in this respect was a tactician's brilliance and that his strategy was misconceived. He elected, as is well known, to join the battle on the grounds that the plays are first and foremost the embodiment of a lesson, illustrations of a thesis, exercises in moral persuasion; he shared Archer's concern for the plays as messages rather than imaginative creations, and even his assessment of Ibsen's technical achievement—the novelty of which he ascribed to the introduction of 'the discussion'—rests on this assumption. But the suspicion grew with time that this had been a false appreciation of what was vital to defend. What happened if one persisted in holding to Shavian criteria is shown very clearly in Spengler's *Decline of the West* which began to appear in 1923. There Spengler trod the path of Shavian Ibsenism to its terminus, finally arriving at the conclusion that Ibsen would have to be banished to the lumber room, to be taken out and dusted down for the benefit of accredited researchers only. Spengler was another of those who saw the drama of the late nineteenth century primarily as a medium for agitation and debate. He placed Ibsen in a cyclic phase that began with Schopenhauer and ended with Shaw, that included the names of Proudhon and Comte, Hebbel and Feuerbach, Marx and Engels, Wagner and Nietzsche, Darwin and John Stuart Mill, the creed of which he defined as 'ethical socialism'. As for the plays themselves, he considered they were so tied to their own age that they would never be able to claim the attention of later generations; their merits, such as they were, were historical rather than intrinsic. By 1950, asserted Spengler confidently, Ibsen will be quite dead.

But although the ideas of Shavian Ibsenism are nowadays generally discredited, its influence on some Ibsen criticism is still potent. Few are any longer misled into it but many are still misled by it, provoked by it into views that are different but equally unacceptable. One imagines the argument going something like this: Ibsen is after all, on all the evidence, not dead but on the contrary very much alive; yet the things he wrote about, the themes, the ideas, the content of the works, no longer seem to concern us very closely; therefore surely his continued vitality can only be ascribed to his technique. It is not what he said, seemingly, but the way he said it. What indeed, it was once asked by H. L. Mencken, are those once famous ideas?

That it is unpleasant and degrading for a wife to be treated as a mere mistress and empty-head; that professional patriots . . . are frauds; that success in business usually involves doing things that a self-respecting man hesitates to do; that a woman who continues to cohabit with a syphilitic husband may expect to have defective children; . . . that a neurotic and lascivious woman is apt to be horrified when she finds that she is pregnant; . . . that the world is barbarously cruel to a woman who has violated the Seventh Commandment or a man who has violated the Eighth.

Such remarks, which are of course meant to be in defence of Ibsen, claim a timelessness for his ideas only by insisting that they are unremarkable. The ideas are considered as neither adding to nor detracting from the real merit of the plays as honest, workman-like, journeyman drama. The consequence is that Ibsen has often found himself in post-Shavian criticism taken out of the company of Schopenhauer, Darwin and Nietzsche and associated rather with Scribe and Augier and Feuillet and Dumas *fils* and the tradition of the *pièce bien faite*; he is respected as one who found a successful solution to certain technical problems of dramatic composition.

It is the swing of the pendulum. Whereas the generation of Holbrook Jackson admired Ibsen as a man 'whose method of criticizing conventional morals by means of drama had a pro-found effect upon thinking people', the present generation is in-clined rather to echo the words of the Angus Wilson character in *Hemlock and After*, who says: 'I admire Ibsen's stagecraft, but I find it more and more difficult to sit through hours of life in the raw.' His moral stock has slumped, but this has been balanced by the appreciation in the value attached to his craftsmanship; he maintains his position, it seems, although no longer as a leader of opinion but rather as a technician of the highest order. And a new orthodoxy bemoans the fact that such a talented writer lavished his gifts on such sadly perishable material.

Yet even Shaw, in the most confidently assertive book ever written about Ibsen, disarmingly admitted the folly of making confident assertion: 'When you have called Mrs. Alving an emancipated woman or an unprincipled one, Alving a debauchee or a victim of society, Nora a fearless and noble-hearted woman or a shocking little liar and an unnatural mother, Helmer a selfish hound or a model husband and father, according to your bias, you have said something which is at once true and false, and in both cases perfectly idle.' This is no less true of the conflicting things that have been said about Ibsen himself; and it echoes a phrase from his own *Emperor and Galilean* first isolated and applied to Ibsen by one of his contemporaries in 1873 and equally valid today: 'What he is, that he is not, and what he is not, that he is'—a phrase of which the critical literature on Ibsen is in its totality an enactment. The first denials came with what the Ibsenites in their day said to those who felt that they knew only too well what Ibsen was; and having established to their own satisfaction what Ibsen was, were themselves in turn rebuked in the same terms. The landscape of his authorship, once mapped by them as a high central plateau of problematic realism, a region peopled with pillars of society and enemies of the people and ghosts, approached through the bewildering thickets of *Brand* and *Peer Gynt* and falling away 'down among the dead men'— this landscape in more recent and more audacious reports is seen as one having as its main feature a triumphantly flowing poetic inspiration, moving in subterranean passages in mid-career, but emerging with enhanced power and sweep in its later reaches.

It becomes increasingly obvious that his genius is of a kind that demands a ceaseless, Forth Bridge-like surveillance, of which it is then meaningless to ask if it is complete but only what point it has reached: whether it is for the moment looking to the 'problems' or to the 'poetic vision'; whether it is concerned with the investigation of 'real people in real situations' or of certain themes, in the enunciation of which the characters are rather the central elements. Whether one calls his dramas the encoded abuse of a fugitive from humiliation, or the occasions for release of private passion, or the night thoughts of one who feared the light, or an audacious and defiant minority report on life; whether one interprets them as the fruits of a mind subtly elated by a sense of secret power or nagged by the possibility that on Sirius two and two might make five; whether one stamps them as visionary or inquisitorial, gnomic or punitive, venomous or intro- spective—the result is to draw too particular a distinction, is to make assertions that are all equally true, equally false, equally idle.

One thing inevitably emerges from any closer study of Ibsen, something rather unsettling to critical orthodoxy; and this is the realization that he does not seem to react very satisfactorily to any of the standard laboratory tests of criticism; further, that any account of his work that limits itself to what is positive and obtrusive in it seems destined to end in triteness; or else—some- thing which is strange and astonishing in this seemingly so straightforward and uncomplicated author—it turns out that any generalization once made seems to demand reservation and quali- fication so drastic that the end result is little short of flat contra- diction. Considerations of this kind lend significance to that other expression of admiration of the 1890s, less strident than the official Ibsenism, less partisan, less conspicuous but more durable and one suspects more influential in a rather indirect way—an admiration of which the defining figure is Henry James. To his friend Elizabeth Robins, one of the greatest Ibsen actresses of the decade, he once wrote: 'What an old boy is our Northern Henry. He is too delightful—an old darling.' What Ibsen might have meant to James personally is suggested by the entry in his Notebooks for 21 December 1896:

I realize—none too soon—that the *scenic* method is my absolute, my imperative, my *only* salvation. The march of an action is the only thing for me to, more and more, attach myself to: it is the only thing that really, for *me*, at least, will *produire* L'ŒUVRE, and L'ŒUVRE is, before God, what I am going in for. Well, the scenic scheme is the only one *I* can trust, with my tendencies, to stick to the march of an action. How reading Ibsen's splendid John Gabriel a day or two ago (in proof) brought that, FINALLY AND FOREVER, home to me!

James's rather ambivalent admiration for Ibsen as it found ex- pression in certain articles of his—one in June 1891 for the *New*

Review on *Hedda Gabler* and another for the *Pall Mall Gazette* in February 1893 on *The Master Builder*, together with two shorter pieces from January and February 1897 in *Harper's Weekly* on *Little Eyolf* and *When We Dead Awaken*—is generally indifferent to those aspects of the dramas his contemporaries considered most worthy of remark; and it is also obvious that whilst he was impressed by Ibsen's technical mastery, it was not to this exclusively that he looked. There was, however, one thing that quite evidently bewildered him; commenting on what he called Ibsen's 'irritating, his bewildering incongruities', he went on: 'He is nothing as a literary personality if not positive; and yet there are moments when his great gift seems made up of negatives, or at any rate when the total seems a contradiction of each of the parts.' There is reinforcement for this idea also in the words of one of Ibsen's more recent critics, Miss M. C. Bradbrook, who when considering *The Wild Duck* writes: 'One day it will be read as a tragedy, the next as the harshest irony; parts of it are clumsy. . . . So searching and yet so delicate is the touch that these flaws and vagaries seem in themselves to strengthen the work.'

Both these expressions of view—that a positive is in part made up of negatives, that weaknesses contribute to strength—seem to put certain qualities in Ibsen in an entirely new light. An absence of humour, an absence of free imagination, an absence of glamour, an absence of what is loosely called 'style' even, add up to nothing; but in the case of Ibsen they seem to multiply up to what has very suitably been called his 'spell'. It seems that you cannot mark him independently on, say, content and style with any hope that a conflation of the two assessments will give any adequate index of his achievement. The constituent elements in his drama are not items in a ledger but factors in a product; his technical skill not an additive but rather an exponent in the algebraic sense, his dramas an exponential series in which the plus and minus quantities function in a way altogether different from those that figure in an accountant's statement of profit and loss. One is encouraged to look at the dramas again, to look not at what is positive and obtrusive but at what is (so to speak) conspicuously

unobtrusive and even assertively negative. One asks oneself
whether this is the occasion to remember the positive significance
of the nil return. Should one approach Ibsen as an occasion not
for counting the heads but for calling the roll, where it is not the
crude total that signifies but rather the meaningful silences and
the absence of response? Always remembering, however, that
those who seem to be playing truant may all the time be hiding
behind the what-not or under the horse-hair sofa.

In the first place there are a number of things that are there
but do not show. This is partly the case with his alleged lack of
humour. There *is* humour there of a kind and there in abundance,
but it is the solitary, unshared, suppressed laughter behind a
desperately straight face; there is the tight-lipped fun that he
made of contemporary Norwegian society, there is the encoded
satire that he aimed at some of his more eminent contemporaries,
a code which a study of the draft manuscripts, the letters and the
life of the author help to crack; and not least there is the wry
ironic detachment with which he turned many a private hurt into
a public show. Nor is it so very different with his alleged lack of
poetry or imaginative inventiveness. So often one hears the reproach that he is prosaic, uncompromisingly realistic, in-
veterately observed—a reproach that admittedly sees (say) *Pillars
of Society* or *An Enemy of the People* or *Ghosts* as the purest and
most characteristic expression of Ibsen's genius, and which is
made only after uneasy glances over the shoulder at the luxuriant
fantasy of *Peer Gynt*. In the matter of poetic content, one is once
again dealing not with some innate deficiency, not with some
lack of aptitude, but with a deliberate act of suppression or con-
cealment. In middle life, after the completion of *Brand* and *Peer
Gynt*, Ibsen took his resolve to renounce poetry in all its more
extravagant or self-conscious forms, to avoid metre, to speak in
the language of men talking to men; it was, as it were, the Preface
to the *Lyrical Ballads* screwed up another notch. But the poetic
vision was not so easily denied; the consequence was a poetry
not of a surface beauty but of inner strength, not of fleshy contour
but of bony structure, of controlled organization without any
concession to prettiness or adornment, and as such it is something

surprisingly modern in its assumptions about poetic communication.

As an architect of drama, Ibsen built with the materials of his age; he displays to view a great deal of grey, massive, solid masonry; but at the same time he appears to be doing astonishing things with his conventional material, to be reaching heights of sublime humdrum, to be performing abnormal feats of normality, to be operating within a style of extravagant sobriety. At times his drama seems tremendously firm and monumental, at other times recklessly audacious and top-heavy; it is only on closer inspection, when one has worked out the hidden architecture, that one realizes how extraordinarily steely it all is, how spendthrift even in its strength. When one looks at the plans, sees from the drafts and sketches (especially of some of the later plays) the meticulous process of re-designing that went on, one realizes that behind and within the outer cladding there is concealed a frame of invention of the highest tensile strength; one discovers not only the pillars of load-bearing realism but also a steel skeleton of poetic imagination. One sees how he shored up the fabric with further devices: buttresses of precise and meaningful stage-direction, scaffoldings of symbolism, motifs that appear decorative but which on examination are discovered also to be taking part of the strain, until the whole thing is braced and strutted into complete rigidity. Only thus was Ibsen able to use so imaginatively such unimaginative language, to compose dialogue that is so unnaturally natural, to make such a vivid impression with creations so uncompromisingly monochrome. It was none other than Maeterlinck—one of the least likely, it might seem, to find anything congenial in Ibsen—who detected this hidden thing; he listened to what he called 'the inner dialogue', those exchanges conducted unspoken behind the spoken word, so eloquently inarticulate.

These dramas suppress their poetry as Brand suppressed his love, and from the same wilful strength. What is love (another of those things so conspicuously absent in Ibsen), says Brand with bitter scorn, but a cloak under which men conceal their lack of will; and what indeed, one might further ask, is hate in these plays but love turned sour—'If Mrs. Borkman had not loved her husband,' Ibsen wrote in explanation of this figure of hate, 'she would have forgiven him long ago.' It seems that absence, and absence alone, makes the heart grow fonder, as one learns from Solveig's example, or from that of Martha in *Pillars of Society*; conversely, the closer the relationship, the more inevitable and bitter the estrangement. How loveless a thing is marriage in Ibsen's world: like Mrs. Alving's to be endured in shame; like Hedda Gabler's, a career in frustration; like the Master Builder's; even the children, Oswald, Hedvig, Little Eyolf, are blighted. There is infatuation in this world, possessiveness, appetite, there is amiability, reasonableness, devotion even; but one will search in vain for any love scene of genuine proportions, for any delicate exploration of personality by two people growing fond of each other.

What of those other deliberately contrived absences, those bare patches in the landscape that were not just left unpopulated but depopulated by design, empty spaces not just left out but carved out? There is in particular that fatal lack which disables the lives of so many of the characters, their essentially negative potential, by which as the result of some insufficiency, some incompetency, some impotence or inherent disqualification, some inauthenticity in the control or direction of their lives, they are so to speak debarred. Never has there been a gallery of lives so dedicated and yet so flawed, so disciplined and yet so unfulfilled, so determined and yet so insensible; lives so dedicated to All or Nothing, to homes for humans, to the good of society, to freedom under responsibility, to the compact majority, finding answers everywhere but in their own hearts; lives that under the pressure of dramatic event reveal (to use Eric Bentley's phrase) not unexpected depths but unexpected shallows.

They are, shall one say, shut away—but from what? From fortune? from happiness? from the truth? from self-fulfilment? Should one for the moment rather say: from the Light? Think of the imprisoned ones: like Hedda in the stuffy cell of her marriage to Tesman, a captive to bumbling amiability, dreaming of an admirer with vine leaves in his hair, and of the thrill of beautiful death; like Nora, placed under doll's house arrest, sneaking a few forbidden macaroons and squandering her life in deceiving her indulgent warder; like Oswald, kept in the dark about his wastrel father the whole of his young life and moaning for the sun; or like Borkman pacing up and down in his gallery like a caged animal. Think also of those who take refuge in a darkness of their own creating, who dwell in the shadow of a phrase or a lie or a secret dream: like Hjalmar Ekdal, comforted by the thought of the photographic invention he will never make; like Consul Bernick, sitting snug in the illusion that he is serving the community; like Alfred Allmers, sustained by the grandiose scheme of writing a big book on Human Responsibility. And here already one can see something that is strongly characteristic of Ibsen's dramatic utterances: the Light is something to play both hide *and* seek with; the Dark is either a prison or a refuge, something that shuts in or shuts out. On the other hand there are those words of Brand who tells of certain ideas (recurrent in Ibsen) that used to send him into fits of laughter: what if an owl were afraid of the dark, or a fish afraid of water? How they would long for 'air and the glad flames of day'. And yet this (he says) is the lot of humankind, living between the fact of having to bear and the realization that it is unbearable; imprisoned. But then the Light, as well as being something to be yearned for, can also be something to be feared. In an early poem of Ibsen called 'Fear of the Light', he confesses that his courage drains away as the sun rises, that the troubles of the day and the claims of life drip cold terror into his heart so that he hides himself under a flap of the scare-crow veil of the dark, embracing night as a protective shield.

Ibsen's benighted are thus of two main kinds: those who long for release, from oppressive respectability, from the common-place, from frustration, who yearn for something wonderful to happen; and those others who take refuge from the insistent demands of life, who build up an insulation against the torments of decision and the agonies of conscience, whose approach to life is a retreat from it, a withdrawal into a stronghold of personal fantasy. And between them stand those who try to fill the fatal

deficiency in their lives by taking from others, who illuminate
their careers with borrowed light; those who apply themselves
earnestly to the business of living but are inherently disqualified,
who are like the African Magician in the Aladdin myth who covets
the lamp that will assure his fortune but is debarred from seizing
it unaided. Either, like Brand, they adopt some impersonal direc-
tive and live by code or statute because they cannot trust themselves to live by rule of thumb; or like Skule, whose sense of
uncertainty is such that he doubts the very doubt that nags him
and who takes over the 'kingly thought' from his rival, they carry
their deficiency about with them like a vacuum, desperately trying
to fill it from without; but instead of filling it, they succeed only
in encasing it in a shell of dedication, fastidiousness or borrowed
authority; each stroke of the drama exhausts this vacuum a little
more until at last the protective shell crumples under the pressure
of external event.

What follows from this realization? The first thing is that these
negative aspects of his work contribute materially to its achievement. It is certainly in part a technical *tour de force*, for it is in
its own way as difficult to incorporate absent qualities in drama
as it is to give examples of them in criticizing it. But it is also
more. When Ibsen writes of the Light as something to yearn for
and to flee from, of the Dark as something that oppresses and
something that comforts, when he regards buildings as being
both homes and cages, he is saying on the level of symbols what
his dramas are often concerned to say dramatically: truth in
Pillars of Society brings salvation, in *The Wild Duck* it brings
destruction; a lie is synonymous with both an ideal and an
illusion, something which for Hjalmar Ekdal makes life tolerable
but which for Consul Bernick makes life intolerable. To ask for
the essence of Ibsen, still more for the quintessence of Ibsenism,
is to formulate a wholly misleading question; there is nothing to
be got by boiling down, there is no extract of wisdom that would
allow us to regard his drama as a linctus for the ills of mankind.
If one must have an analogy, one might be a little nearer the
truth by asking for the root of Ibsen; for just as the root of (say)
9 is not 3 but that more ambiguous entity mathematicians call

±3, so the root of Ibsen's view of life, however positively he may at times seem to express himself, conveys the impression of being similarly 'plus or minus'. The separate bits may not add up very satisfactorily, but they function.

The problem is then what sort of questions the modern Ibsenite should ask. One notices that in an age when literature gave itself to the business of debate, Ibsen himself waited for question time and cast his dramas in an interrogative mould. 'I do but ask,' he was fond of saying to those who sought enlightenment from him about the meaning of his works, 'my call is not to answer'. His dramas are those of one who understood the strategy of the contrived question and the shrewd supplementary, who knew how much more could be achieved by implication and insinuation and by the manner and timing of the asking than by the mere forcing of some answer. Perhaps his critics could learn from his example and acknowledge that there is room for an approach to Ibsen that questions the questions we ask of him rather than competes for answers. He offers a problem in delicate handling in which the matter of whether questions can be found to yield definite answers is subordinate to that of finding a genuinely Ibsenite question with the rightly provocative degree of obliquity. For example: Is there any Thing that might be discovered as standing to Ibsen as the Wild Duck stands to *The Wild Duck*?

Contemplating such Ibsenist Things, one wonders: How symbolic are they, and how are they symbolic, and are they all symbolic in the same way—the Wild Duck, the white horses in *Rosmersholm*, the sea in *The Lady from the Sea*, the 'Indian Girl' in *Pillars of Society*, the infected baths, the orphanage, the high towers in *An Enemy of the People*, *Ghosts* and *The Master Builder*? What at one time it was sufficient to call a symbol (whether or not one felt inclined to add, like Arnold Bennett, 'deplorable, even in its ingenuity') is now a 'symbol', shielded by its quotation marks from any simple view that it might 'stand for' anything in some straightforward sense; it is sometimes credited with explanatory or elucidatory power, sometimes with cohesive or magnetic force; at times it is seen as 'a pressure point for all kinds of feeling', at times as a kind of appliance which gathers 'all the scattered lights of the play and focuses them in one'; there is some suspicion that it is often attached to its play (and therefore 'detachable') rather than inherently of it, that it is centrally placed rather than nuclear, perhaps even that it is intrinsic and extrinsic at one and the same time.

The Wild Duck is no doubt in one sense a centre of attraction; but it might be thought to have other and possibly more significant functions as a kind of formula or code word for finding the centre of gravity, the point about which all the separate elements exactly balance one another. Asked to imagine the shape of the play to which it belongs, one might see it as something equivocal, like a boomerang perhaps or a question mark, where the centre of gravity lies not within but without; but if one were to hang it up at any point, at Hedvig, say, or Hjalmar or Old Ekdal or the 'life-lie' and allow things to find their natural equilibrium, this centre of gravity—although nothing more than a point in space— would come to rest immediately below the point of suspension; what one is not able to do is actually *balance* anything on this point of balance, this point which is detached and yet not strictly detachable, which is a function of the configuration of the piece rather than something of a piece with it. It would then be immaterial whether one hung the problem plays uppermost, or the visionary, or the poetic and non-theatrical; a private enthusiasm for, say, *A Doll's House* or *Ghosts* or *Peer Gynt* or even *Emperor and Galilean* (which would probably have been Ibsen's own choice) ought in theory all to point to the same spot.

Staring too fixedly, however, at the Wild Duck has its dangers, and in straining the vision the analogy itself becomes strained. Looking round for a moment instead at the company it keeps, one becomes aware of another bird which has been strangely disregarded, one which along with Chekhov's Seagull seems to be —no matter what ornithology might say—a bird of a feather: Boccaccio's Falcon, that which appears in the ninth story of the fifth day of the *Decameron*. There is even some suggestion that the resemblance is not altogether accidental, the link between the two being Paul Heyse, German critic and author, whom Ibsen met in 1875 while living in Munich. Ibsen frequently attended the weekly meetings of the Crocodile Society, of which Heyse was a prominent member, and they saw much of each other without ever becoming close friends. A few years earlier, in 1871, Heyse had sketched his theory of the *Novelle*, his so-called *Falkentheorie*, derived from a study of Boccaccio's story; and it would be surprising if this did not on some occasion provide the society with something to discuss. Heyse had summed up his argument in the words: 'Der Leser wird sich überall fragen, wo der Falke sei: also das Spezifische, das diese Geschichte von tausend anderen unterscheidet', i.e. look for the falcon, that which in some recognizable but not easily definable way focuses, particularizes, concretizes the work and gives it identity. A simple translation of Heyse's formula provides a paraphrase of the question implied above, a question in which Ibsen might have found quiet amusement, where the inner ramifications are everything and the answers largely incidental: Where is Ibsen's Wild Duck, that which distinguishes him from a thousand others?

The immediate past is not lacking in suggestions, many of which resemble each other only in their determination not to flatter. For James Joyce's Stephen Dedalus the differentia was cathartic: 'You have,' he said to the Ibsenite, 'connected Ibsen and Eno's fruit salt for ever in my mind.' For Arne Garborg it was demonic, suggesting to him the figure of Trollman Whitebeard who spoke in riddles and acted so wise and turned the whole country into a madhouse by his magic. For Sir Walter Raleigh it was swinish: 'I send you Zola and Ibsen', he wrote in a letter accompanying two very ugly cabinet photographs, '. . . they seem to me to embody modern earnestness, crankiness, gloom and stupidity in their speaking countenances. . . . I think we must frame them with the legend "Modern Pigs" underneath.' And Ibsen himself provided ammunition for his detractors by his reference to the Scorpion which preserved its health by injecting its poison into a piece of soft fruit: 'Is there not a similarity,' he wrote, 'between this and writing poetry?' Many of the lyric poems, as well as the dramas themselves, make a contribution to the discussion, embodying in particular many of those more obvious and generally acknowledged qualities of their author: the profound and wholly pitiless psychological insight, the complex subtleties of organization, the stern judgement of individual responsibility, the scorn of inauthentic living and thinking. In the poems, the Strange Hunter on the *vidda* forces mortals to contemplate their lives 'steel-set'; the Miner hammers his way into the secret chambers of the heart, ever deeper, seeking the answer to life's riddle, forgoing even the consolation of the light; and there is the suggestion of the Judge who holds doom sessions on the soul. Ibsen's astonishing technical skill invited identification with the Master Builder; and in view of Rubek's sardonic remarks in *When We Dead Awaken*, this might well be extended to include also a Master Sculptor:

There is something equivocal, something hidden within and behind these portraits—something private that the others cannot see. . . . I alone can see it. And I find it intensely amusing. Superficially there's the 'striking likeness', as it is called, that people all stand gaping at in astonishment—but deeper down it is . . . just the dear old barnyard.

Nor should one neglect the Amazingly Clever Dog, the one that in any case fished up the Wild Duck from the depths—a Dog who (to put too fine a point on it, no doubt) was at first treated like a cur but lived to have the day the proverb promised him, who was fierce and bristling but who, if tossed a decoration by some crowned head, could be placated.

All these things are, however, too partial, too explicit, too 'symbolic' in the sense that the Wild Duck is not; and when they are asked to accommodate some of the other less obvious but no less pervasive elements in these dramas, they fail. Where is the relevance to the incessant self-analysis of those characters who, as Hofmannsthal said, are forever thinking about thinking, feeling themselves feeling and conducting autopsychology; who think in slogans and long for the miraculous; who decorate their egocentric lives with secret dreams, subordinating all about them in private illusions of grandeur; whose lives are the deeds they have left undone, whose speech is the words they have left unspoken? Nor is it without relevance that these are explanations one makes in the study and not in the theatre; and many sensitive critics have insisted that it is only in the theatre that Ibsen should properly be judged. It is not good, they suggest, to go trudging down long avenues of reference every time Ibsen points his finger; there is, in the theatre, no time for digression, the pace has to be maintained. This was the view of James Joyce, whose early enthusiasm for Ibsen led him to teach himself Norwegian, the better to read the plays, who in March 1901 in his newly acquired foreign tongue wrote to Ibsen a very moving letter of homage and admiration, and who in an enthusiastic article on *When We Dead Awaken* in the *Fortnightly Review* of April 1900 claimed that 'appreciation, hearkening, is the only true criticism':

If any plays demand a stage they are the plays of Ibsen. . . . They are so packed with thought. At some chance expression, the mind is tortured with some question, and in a flash long reaches of life are opened up in vista, yet the vision is momentary unless we stay to ponder it. It is just to prevent excessive pondering that Ibsen requires to be acted.

The real answer seems to be therefore that there is no answer; or rather that there is an infinity of answers too stark and stiff to fit anywhere but where they touch—which makes the modern Ibsenites' search for enlightenment a matter not of discovering some single secret truth but of rejecting a multiplicity of explanations which under scrutiny turn out to be inadmissible. Not even the precise ambiguity of the paradox nor the ambiguous precision of the 'symbol' serve in the last resort to break down the complex unity of his art; he is irreducible.

* 6 *

BJØRNSTJERNE BJØRNSON

'It was not laziness that caused the delay,' wrote Bjørnson in 1858 to explain why his story *Arne* had taken so long to finish, 'but *dissipation of effort*. . . . Naturally, any hint of rebellion in the theatre I had to put down. I have been putting across the opposition case in the press, addressing the merchants' clubs, ditto the workmen's, arguing aesthetics in the papers, writing lyrics for patriotic occasions, preaching Scandinavianism, and the Lord knows what else I haven't done.' And for the rest of his life, the story was always pretty much the same: as theatre director, editor, public speaker, author, journalist and a score of other things besides, he distributed in prodigal fashion the wealth of his astonishing talents. His writings are the enduring elements of a life that was devoted to causes: national, political, social, educational, linguistic, theatrical. He was the supreme Norwegian, he was of his people and for his people, personifying its ideals, articulating its desires, holding it together at a critical time in its history and leading it along by sheer force of personality. Irrepressibly in on everything, he was in all respects a public figure.

A 'public', and the immediate and direct response that he drew from it, meant very much more to Bjørnson than a merely pleasurable accompaniment to living and writing; they were wholly necessary things, lacking which his personality lost a whole dimension, and without which his talents operated at less than full power. It was not 'the gentle reader' he wrote for so much as 'the great reading public'. Indeed for him literature was never 'just' literature; and when in 1907 he looked back over fifty years to the work that had first endeared him to his people

—the novel *Synnøve Solbakken*—he saw no need to disguise what his attitude had been and continued to be towards literary expression: 'Many regarded *Synnøve* as being just a novel, mere *belles lettres*. With *Synnøve*, I intended something more. I did not write merely to make a book. What I wrote was a plea on behalf of those who worked the land. . . . We had come to see that the language of the sagas lived on in them, and that their life lay close to the sagas. The life of our nation was to be built on our history, and now these were the people who were to provide the foundation.' His intent was at its clearest in those things he wrote before 1872, the time of his so-called 'crop-rotation' working, in which narrative works alternated with dramatic: the *Peasant Tales* on the one hand with their contemporary themes and their happy endings; and on the other the dramas, saga-inspired and tragic. In both, the design deliberately stressed those links that bound the new Norway to the old; and by creating, in his stories especially, an image of Norwegian life that was like enough to be recognizable but idealized enough to constitute an incentive, he was doing exactly what his Swiss contemporary Gottfried Keller had urged: 'Just as one confronts pregnant women with beautiful works of art, so one must always exhibit to the ever-pregnant national stock something better than it really is.' Thus it would, he claimed, come to be what it vaguely imagined itself to be, but was not. Even when his work appears unexpectedly reticent or detached, it is still the manifestation of a talent essentially rhetorical in kind. Extroverted, confident, impassioned, Bjørnson knew his own people as an orator knows his audience, knew its sympathies, sensed its deeper desires and led it where in some obscure but deeply felt way it wanted to go. He was quick to leap to the support of the underprivileged, and ready to thunder against what he felt to be the culpable inertia of entrenched authority; he was all for educational opportunity, all for women's emancipation, for tolerance; he was conspicuous in his championing of all that was decent.

Of this essentially public figure, his letters to his wife Karoline give a private view. But with Bjørnson, one must at once beware: these intimate snap-shots are, in some not very easily explicable

way, less candid than those other more carefully composed portraits by which he has hitherto been known; in these unrehearsed
gestures it is as though he were doing what came unnaturally;
only the pose is real. He who fancies he can strip off some supposedly artificial public *persona*, beneath which the real Bjørnson
might be found, altogether misunderstands the nature of the
man. Rather the contrary is true: that here one is dealing with
a personality that was never genuinely complete, never wholly
fulfilled, never quite spontaneously itself until others had made it
so by their focused attention and the unison of their response.
An audience was to him what a context is to the telling word:
a defining thing giving meaning.

This explains a number of things. It explains why he often
could not resist putting on the oratorical manner for what were
quite private occasions, such as when his fifth child was born and
he addressed his wife like a public meeting:

Dear friend, fecund wife, proud mother of a fifth child, three boys
and two girls; who five times has endured the mortal struggle to bring
increase to our line—five times kissed your own issue for the first time,
thanking the Almighty for His favour! And my name you have borne
with you in your pain as in your thanks, and my image came upon you
in the hour of creation, and you kissed it with rapture as it quickened
to life. Blessed woman, heavy with love, eager for sacrifice, I thank you
by all that I live for, all my power to love and to believe. By the rich
fruitfulness of your being is Heaven mirrored in our minds, your
journies to the frontiers of life bring a sense of its seriousness into our
alliance, diminish what is bad and render our daily life more precious,
our duties greater, and yet our joys nobler and more numerous.

A second consequence is that many of his judgements within
this private sphere seem completely untypical of Bjørnson, seem
bereft of those larger qualities that characterized his public
utterances. Being himself a man of hugely generous impulses, he
was angered by anything he felt was niggling or small-minded;
and it is not difficult to share his impatience in many cases, such
as the occasion when he suffered at the tongues of the bigoted,
gossiping society of Bergen in 1871: 'God how petty everything
is here, Karoline, full of prejudice, gossip, lies and much worse

even than Kristiania.' 'Petty' is a word that recurs in his denunciations, like a cue for applause. But how unlike Bjørnson it seems when he applies this same word to Paris in 1863:

The French are altogether incomparably petty. Take first their language: an endless affair of petty sophistries and affectations. For this reason their literature is almost inaccessible for a foreigner. The design of their daily life is a web of pettiness than can only shock the Scandinavian mind. Their view of life is petty. . . . Walking in the streets, you never see a single respectable face in the whole district; for the middle classes who have their businesses there are immoral; man and woman, immoral to a degree we never dream of. . . . I am like a man who longs for pure air. Everything I see and hear and breathe is impure.

In spite of the art galleries and museums, in spite of the life of the theatre, in spite of its cosmopolitan atmosphere, he was bored with Paris, he wrote. And the Nordic self-righteousness of his censure is—even after full allowance is made for his having been travel-weary and anxious to be back with his wife—quite insufferable. Until, that is, one realizes how unreliable is the nature of the testimony these letters give.

The intriguing and in one sense alarming thing, however, is to see how certain habits, certain actions, certain principles of conduct which on the purely private level are often little more than fads become in public a kind of proclamation or assertion, a heroic and symbolic deed. Consider his cult of the vigorous life and his passion for personal cleanliness. In his letters from America in 1880 and 1881, he kept telling his wife how he always slept with his window wide open with several degrees of frost outside; and how it was also his habit to rise at six and wash himself all over with a sponge and American soap before his early morning walk—unexceptionable habits that turn faddish only when he goes on to inquire about the bathing habits of his sons at home: 'Tell me, does he [Bjørn, the eldest] wash his entire body every day with a big sponge and soap? Get him to do this, and buy a sponge for Ejnar at the same time.' With the prospect of an audience of sorts, however, such unremarkable ways took on a more splendid magnificence. Richard le Gallienne has described how in the 1890s he and a companion arrived one morning very early at Bjørnson's house in the country and were met by their host, 'with his leonine head and great shaggy white hair, awaiting us, his arms stretched out in welcome, like a patriarch.' Bjørnson had his bath towel over his shoulder, and he invited his visitors to join him in the woods:

It was an heroic welcome, but we were game, and presently the three of us were tramping through the woods till we came to where a mountain stream fell in a torrent of white water down the face of a rock. . . . 'This is my shower bath,' said Bjørnson, as he stripped, and there presently he stood, firm as a rock, beneath the cataract, the water pouring over his strong shoulders, his white head white as the foam, and shouting with joy of the morning. So might some great old water-god have stood and laughed amid the sun-flashing spray. It was a picture of elemental energy never to be forgotten. . . .

Undeniably—as le Gallienne's report so surely betrays—Bjørnson loved an audience. But it would be profoundly misleading to leave the statement at that, as though suggesting that such occasions meant nothing more to him than the opportunity for exhibitionism. Between a Bjørnsonian act done privately and its comparable public enactment there were differences that were always subtle, often profound, and rarely the mere consequence of a change of scale or setting. To any performer, an audience is a stimulant; to his ideas, an amplifier; but in Bjørnson's case there was something much more significant and much more mysterious than either of these things: and that was the unique way in which the simple fact of there being any public occasion at all altered the nature and the value of what was said and done. To confront Bjørnson with an audience was to create conditions whereby what might otherwise have been a private platitude became a profound public truth, where the heroic was revealed in the trivial, and a personal fetish charged with deep symbolic meaning.

In each of the three earlier 'Peasant Tales' which appeared between 1857 and 1860, *Synnøve Solbakken*, *Arne* and *A Happy*

Boy (*En glad Gut*), the basic pattern is identical: the tracing of a career from childhood through suffering and tearful experience to wedding bells. Bjørnson himself confessed to writing the final pages of *Synnøve Solbakken* with tears in his eyes; and any statistical count of the vocabulary of these stories would surely give the verb 'to weep' a high rating. Tears of sorrow, tears of joy, manly tears, red eyes, sniffs and choking sobs are never long absent; Arne's mother cannot see to read 'for she had wept so much in her time'. 'She weeps so easily', says Synnøve's mother at one point, and the reader nods his agreement. Yet it would be false to interpret this as a sign of cheap sentimentality; the insistence on tears is unexpectedly a corollary of one of the real merits of Bjørnson's narrative: the depth of feeling communicated by the very reticence of his characters. There is in many of the situations a genuine and, as it were, 'built-in' pathos, and the characters are at the mercy of strong emotion which they do not fully comprehend, and which is defined by the nature of the dilemma and not by any analysis or verbal formulation; even in some situations not far short of the melodramatic, there is a terse understatement in the conversational exchanges that is wholly in keeping with the nature of the characters and their experience, and which holds the narrative taut. Deep feeling is something that inhibits speech; and conversely, this same inarticulateness is a thing that drives the feeling deeper. The unhappiness of Baard, 'this lumbering but fundamentally decent man', is that of one who suffers dumbly because he lacks the tongue to justify his well-intentioned but disastrous actions; and when, after twenty-one years of unhappily married life, he is reconciled with his wife, the words come only with difficulty: 'Both had something to say, but it was expressed only by their both standing there in silence.' Tears are the only concession to reticence, a sign only of the emotion that lies in what they do *not* say.

This taciturnity is, however, compensated for by the often logically improbable but aesthetically well-conceived introduction of passages of pure lyric poetry, a device which, however, is lacking in the last of his 'Peasant Tales', *The Bridal March* (*Brude-Slaatten*), written in 1872. Without the relief of this formal eloquence, these stories would have little more than the strong and urgent simplicity of a vintage Western where, against a background of wild but essentially unhostile nature, the men are tight-lipped, the women weep, and drink is a ubiquitous evil. The element that one sadly misses in these stories is some kind of good-humoured irony, the very quality that Keller's tales, for example, are so rich in. One feels indeed that, had it not been that the author loved his characters too well, these stories might easily have had tragic instead of happy endings; the seeds of tragedy are often there in the characters, and the logic of the action often seems to point in that direction; but Bjørnson's artistic detachment was overwhelmed by his affection for those he was writing of. The only surprising thing is that some contemporary criticism should have thought these works too 'raw'; modern opinion thinks rather the reverse.

In the saga-dramas that complemented these tales, the achievement was more varied. Taking 'national pride' as the attitude common to both the tales and the dramas, there is more than a suspicion that, whereas in the tales it was tempered by love, in the dramas it was fanned by envy. Bjørnson himself admitted how a trip in 1856 to Uppsala and Stockholm, with their visible monuments of a great and glorious past, aroused his 'historical envy'; and it was his wish that the Norwegian people similarly should know and cherish their own great historical traditions. Partly because the element of pride thus became a little strident, partly because the reticence that Bjørnson had accepted as typical of the Norse spirit posed greater technical difficulties in the way of dramatic treatment than it would in the narrative, the dramas do not always carry full conviction: *Between the Battles* (*Mellem slagene*), remodelled from a contemporary theme in fourteen days on his return from Sweden in 1856, is not wholly ineffective as a piece of self-dramatization in the figure of King Sverre; but *Lame Hulda* (*Halte-Hulda*) and *King Sverre* (*Kong Sverre*), which followed in the next two years, are weak; the trilogy *Sigurd Slembe*, completed in 1862, is admirable in its technical sureness, but it is its eternal misfortune to have to bear comparison with Ibsen's *The Pretenders* (which appeared in the following year), and in spite of its attempt to treat deep moral problems, it lacks the intellectual profundity of Ibsen's work; in its command of the historical perspectives, however, and in its technical discipline, it bears comparison with Schiller's *Wallenstein*, which, incidentally, Bjørnson greatly admired. (Some stimulus from Schiller might also be detected in Bjørnson's excursion into English history in the drama *Mary Queen of Scots* (*Maria Stuart i Skotland*) written in 1864.) Finally there was *Sigurd Jorsalfar* in 1872, which with its complement *King Eystejn* (*Kong Eystejn*, published posthumously in 1932) marked the completion of this phase of his dramatic activities.

In all these dramas, the motives determining the actions of the characters are elemental and undifferentiated, the situations *allgemein menschlich*. In the case of the women, love rules all; in the case of the men, power; these are the categorical imperatives, these the daemonic powers deep in their nature that they are powerless to disobey. Inga, in *Between the Battles*, abandons husband, home and family to follow her lover; Hulda clings to her husband's murderer in defiance of society's laws; they and their sisters in these dramas are prey to the overwhelming passion that breaks down all reserves, drowns any voice of conscience, defeats all convention; this is their all or nothing in a society that offers no other avenue of self-fulfilment, and makes of their love a desperate thing. The men of these dramas are heroic, but in a Viking rather than a Greek sense; physical strength is as much a part of the complete man as moral fearlessness; they are impelled by motives of ambition, of personal power, as often as not into mortal conflict with their nearest kin; and it is part of the masculine principle in these works that the men can find only momentary satisfaction in the happiness of a life *à deux*. Inevitably then the dramatic conflicts—the one tending towards jealousy, and the other towards revenge—are so to speak coupled in series rather than in parallel: woman seeks fulfilment in man, and man among men; she seeking by her love to bind him to her, he seeking release that he might bind his fellows to him by fear and respect. Any problems, any misgivings they may severally have are nevertheless of the same order—how far they

may go and what means they may employ to achieve their ends
—but they terminate at different points.

One acknowledges, however, two exceptions to these generalizations: in *Mary Queen of Scots* the traditional roles of man and
woman are reversed, with the ruthless and ambitious Mary displaying the more obviously masculine characteristics, and the
weak Darnley representing the forces of eroticism and jealousy;
and in *Sigurd Slembe* Bjørnson has created in the figure of Harald
Jarl a character of subtle modernity, a man who, though humili-
ated and banished by his half-brother, finds any thought of
revenge or of the re-acquisition of power wholly distasteful, who
wins a brief happiness from life through his friendship with a
young boy, and who is sickened by the plots of those who seek
his reinstatement.

The changes initiated by the two plays of 1875, *A Bankrupt*
(*En Fallit*) and *The Editor* (*Redaktøren*)—plays which not only
introduced the realistic problem drama into Scandinavia but also
carried Bjørnson's personal fame beyond the frontiers of Norway
to Germany and America—were extensive, whilst nevertheless
leaving the fundamentals of his dramatic art largely untouched.
Actually, Bjørnson had made a tentative beginning with a
'modern' drama some ten years previously and the result had
been a play modest in its dimensions but firm in its touch: *The
Newly-married Couple* (*De Nygifte*). Using only five characters,
it took a timeless problem—a husband's break with his rich
parents-in-law and his fight to retain his wife's affection—and
considered it in a modern setting. What is missing, however, is
the element of agitation that informs the later problem dramas,
and it is no surprise to find that Georg Brandes dismissed it as a
play about pale young lovers feeding on milk and water; and it
is rather the year 1875 that marks the ultimate transition in his
work from the historical to the modern, from romanticism to
realism, from the national to the problematical, from 'historical
envy' to righteous indignation, from the themes of peasant life
and traditional heroes to those of urban and commercial affairs
of the contemporary age. Love and power are still the forces that
move his men and women, but there has been a kind of institu-

tionalizing at work: raw passion is replaced by concern for the decencies of matrimony, the naked will to power becomes a reactionary intrigue to preserve it; instinct gives way to expediency, the urgent fearlessness of kings and nobles has become the defensive ruthlessness of ship-owners and company directors, editors and industrialists. The rhetorical gestures are still there; but instead of the arms flung wide as though to embrace and welcome, the finger is pointed in accusation.

Following the pointed finger, one contemplates a series of representative figures whose careers enact their author's optimistic faith in the power of common decency. Consul Tjælde in *A Bankrupt*, the title figure of *The Editor*, as well as Riis, the director-general of *The New System* (*Det ny System*, 1879), all represent the *status quo*; all of them fight a rearguard action, showing much resourcefulness and little integrity, when their positions of power and authority are in jeopardy. But in as much as these three plays tell of the victory of a simple, and largely unarticulated, community good over a private, though socially engendered, evil, they are theatrical rather than dramatic. There is a demonstration of how such modern concentrations of authority tend to corrupt; and there is also an invitation (clear in *A Bankrupt*, less explicit in the other two plays) to see something morally cleansing in being stripped of these modern and unnatural garments of power. Certain institutions of modern society that these figures represent, certain attitudes of mind that they personify, are thus indicted, but the offence is merely sordid; what we have is an accusation, a documenting of the social crime, whereupon justice is done, and seen to be done; but there is no serious clash of personalities, no real thrust in the conflict of ideas, for there is in these plays none of equal stature to oppose or, as it were, cross-examine the delinquents.

It is only considerations such as these that lend significance to Bjørnson's otherwise unremarkable drama, *The King* (*Kongen*), written two years before *The New System* and displaying certain characteristics of dramatic organization that anticipate what is supreme in Bjørnson's drama: *Beyond Our Power* (*Over Ævne, I*) of 1883 and *Paul Lange and Tora Parsberg* of 1898. In *The King* there is the expected attack on selected (and, as Bjørnson thought, ossified) social institutions, especially the monarchy; but on this occasion it is a satirical attack from within, by one who inherits authority and is disquieted by its consequences. Much in the structure of this play might be thought of as being Hebbelian in conception, basing itself on the notion of conflict between the Individual and the Whole, between the isolated progressive or eruptive force and the inertia of things as they are, whereby the individual suffers eclipse. The king who comes to realize that by his position and his power he has been acting a lie, who attempts to bring the established institutions of state and church into line with his own ideals and who is impatient of the empty phrases of the 'pillars of society' who surround him, represents a positive standpoint; he is the dramatic correlative of the ideas Bjørnson expressed later that same year in an address to the Christiania students, called 'To be in Truth'. The king's offence, in contrast to the editor's and the bankrupt's, is sublime; and genuine dramatic force resides in the structure of this play; in its final formulation, however, it merits Arne Garborg's (admittedly qualified) description of it as 'a newspaper article', in spite of the care that Bjørnson lavished on the intermezzo-like scenes between the acts that were meant to redress the balance of poetry and polemic in the work.

Meanwhile, in moving from the timelessness and the even rhythm of the peasant milieu, from 'the narrow confines of parish life', to the more hectic tempo of modern urban society, Bjørnson was also graduating in the field of the narrative from the 'tale' to the novel. *The Fisher Lass* (*Fiskerjenten*, 1868), more than a *Novelle* but something less than a novel, follows the heroine from her modest home to the big city, where her ambition lies with the theatre; in mixing idyllic description with undigested Darwinism and a patient and rather condescending defence of the theatre from a Christian point of view, it is (as with so much of Bjørnson) both charming and irritating at once. *Captain Mansana* (*Kaptejn Mansana*, 1875) is in compass no more than a sketch (its original title was actually 'A sketch from Italy') and gives short rehearsal to a theme that was to inform much of his later work: the un-

wholesome effect of a sick society on one of its members. Nor is
Magnhild (1877) a novel in any complete sense, although perhaps
it deserved to be; for its brevity is not that of disciplined economy
but lack of amplitude, the result of Bjørnson's boredom with it
half-way through its composition. It invites, but does not bear,
comparison with *Madame Bovary*; yet in many ways it reveals a
sharper vision, a lack of sentimentality just a little startling in
Bjørnson's work, and shows that his attitude to peasant life had
undergone a strange and unexpected transformation—'The Lord
preserve us from becoming peasants,' he wrote in a letter shortly
after the publication of *Magnhild*—and that he was now sharply
critical of this way of life.

After the late 1870s, Bjørnson's work entered a kind of vigorous
middle-age, with all the merits and demerits that this implies.
His style shows all the confidence of the mature artist, yet with
all the old élan unimpaired, so that this last period of his authorship contains much of what is undoubtedly his best work; but it
is set in its habits and, as Professor Francis Bull has indicated, all
the works that follow fall conveniently under two headings: those
like the dramas *Leonarda* (1789), *A Gauntlet* (*En Handske*, 1883),
Geography and Love (*Geografi og Kjærlighed*, 1885), *Laboremus*
(1901), *Daglannet* (1904) and *When the New Wine blooms* (*Når den
ny vin blomstrer*, 1909), which along with the narrative works
Dust (*Støv*, 1882) and *The Heritage of the Kurts* (*Det flager i byen
og på havnen*, 1884) deal with private and largely individual
problems, home and marriage, sexual relations, parents and children, the education of the young and the rights of women; and
on the other hand, those like the dramas *Beyond Human Might*
and *Paul Lange and Tora Parsberg* and the novel *In God's Way*
(*Paa Guds veje*, 1889) which treat of the individual's relations
with some supra-personal authority, of the affairs of community
and church, of party and country, of politics and religion, of the
existence of fanaticism and intolerance.

For Bjørnson's women, the way towards greater independence
leads via their discovery of the beastliness of men. *Leonarda* is a
highly contrived drama on the theme of women and divorce, in
which the men either drink, or deceive their wives, or spread

nasty rumours, or marry where there is no longer any love; as a drama, it tends to lose its way in a maze of emotional entanglements, and sacrifices too much to the one supremely theatrical moment when Leonarda triumphs over the bishop: in answer to the allegations that she receives a lover into her house at suspicious times of the day, she reveals that the alleged lover is none other than her own divorced husband! Svava Riis, in *A Gauntlet*, also comes to the conclusion that all men are contemptible with the discovery that her father is an old libertine, her fiancé a young one. In time, however, the women in Bjørnson's plays take their revenge: Karen Tygesen in *Geography and Love* brings her egotistical scholar husband to heel by absenting herself from the household for a few days, in a comedy where Bjørnson treads with great circumspection round the problem of how to keep the wife's motives and behaviour above reproach; in *Daglannet* there is a similar wifely victory over an overbearing husband; whilst in *When the New Wine blooms*, Bjørnson varies the situation by exploiting the same device he had used in *Mary Queen of Scots*: he invests the wife with what had been traditionally the husband's authority, sends her out into the great world of commerce as a career woman, and allows the husband to revenge himself by running off to Australia.

The most beastly of all Bjørnson's men is, however, Kurt (in the novel known in English translation as *The Heritage of the Kurts*) who after the opening chapters nevertheless survives only as a Darwinian threat to the hero, his direct descendent Thomas Rendalen. The situation that serves as a basis for the narrative is wholly Bjørnsonian: the son of a drunken libertine (hereditary influence) is brought up with great caution by his widowed mother under her maiden name (environmental influence) and finds himself in time as headmaster of a girls' school; there he can put into practice, and give long public discourses on, his advanced ideas about women's education. Perhaps this is the novel that one of Knut Hamsun's characters had in mind when moved to remark of Bjørnson that 'his victories are resounding, his mistakes are tremendous'; for the final climax to the action —the wedding march, the unsuspecting bride, the black-veiled schoolgirl friend who is the victim of the bridegroom's lust, the bastard child flung on the altar steps with the cry: 'Will you have it to kneel on?'—must surely be one of the more tremendous of Bjørnson's mistakes. In general, however, the women in these works commend themselves as representatives of their sex rather than as unique or idiosyncratic individuals; they can be counted on to demand an end to their degradation by a society dominated by the male, to seek for educational opportunities and the right to enter the professions, to insist on such sexual restraint from men as is by convention expected from women, and to claim an equal voice not merely in domestic but also in public affairs.

Can it be wholly by chance that Bjørnson was infinitely more successful with that other group of works, of which *Beyond Our Power* is unquestionably the most brilliant? This intensely moving drama of a man who 'hoped too much from Heaven' grew organically through five years of deliberation; incredible though it may seem, it was originally planned as a comedy; then it was nearly re-written as a novel in 1880, and was given its final shape as we know it in 1883. What began as yet another theatre-launched denunciation, ended as a beautifully poised, almost laconic piece in two acts, taut, concentrated, and with a richness of implication that accounts in great measure for its uniqueness in Bjørnson's published work. Elsewhere it is generally only too clear whose side Bjørnson is on, and we are never left in any doubt as to where our sympathies are meant to lie; but here is a play impious in design yet sustained by a great piety, where sceptic and believer appear equally vulnerable, where fanaticism is not without sublimity, where reasonableness seems faintly comic, and where irony never loses its dignity. The object of its attack—for attack it still is, being genuine Bjørnson—is not in this instance some abuse or social malpractice or moral mis-demeanour, but a pernicious attitude of mind, a nimiety or 'too-muchness' which, by its lack of realism in demanding the fulfil-ment of ideals impossible of realization in this imperfect world, serves only to sow deceit and hypocrisy and folly in the minds of men. *Beyond Our Power* reflects Bjørnson's newly-won convic-tion that decency and morality count for more than any officially

Christian faith, and that a belief in the miraculous is unhealthy and remote from life as we know it. Unthinking attachment to such ideals, it seems to say, is merely self-deception on a sublime level if it conflicts with what we must acknowledge as the hard facts of reality. *Beyond Our Power* examined this thesis in the light of evidence from religious doctrine, whilst its companion piece of twelve years later, *Beyond Human Might* (*Over Ævne II*, 1895) scrutinized this same quality of fanatic idealism as it showed itself in the field of revolutionary politics; this latter play overreaches itself, however, is itself a little 'too much', and lacks the controlled power of its predecessor.

The geometry of the novel *In God's Way* is from one point of view quite intricate: the quadrilateral of a man's relationship to his wife, to his sister and to her husband, with a criss-cross of diagonal loyalties and attractions, of passions and friendship and family. But the proposition, of which the novel serves as a proof, is one familiar from *Beyond Our Power*—that true morality and orthodox Christian teaching are concepts that by no means neces- sarily overlap. The personal relationships in the novel are of sub- sidiary importance in comparison with the fact that the two men, parson and doctor, represent two conflicting philosophies, from the clash of which comes a strong plea for tolerance. In construc- tion, this novel is shapelier than *The Heritage of the Kurts* and reveals a certain readiness on Bjørnson's part to reject material that might have halted the onward movement of the narrative; so that there is (as Hamsun said in his review of it) nothing merely routine in it. But any more positive approval of it would have to be hedged round high with reservations. The most impressive proof of Bjørnson's artistic vitality is provided by the drama he completed in 1898, *Paul Lange and Tora Parsberg*; its indictment is of the ways of politics that will ruthlessly and unscrupulously hound to death an opponent for the sake of party gain, its pleas made explicit in the heroine's final words: 'Oh why must it be that the good men so often become martyrs? Will we never reach the stage where they can become leaders?'

Bjørnson is perhaps at his most characteristically Bjørnsonian in his lyric poetry. The first edition of the *Poems and Songs* (*Digte og Sange*) dated from 1870, the fourth and last from 1903; and in view of his reputation as a lyric poet in his own country, it is at first surprising to see how small his output was, the last edition containing only about 140 items. Most of the poems date from before 1875, that is from before his religious crisis; and the fact that his beliefs at that time were orthodoxly Lutheran, tinged with Grundtvigianism, ensures that most of the sentiments expressed in these poems are unexceptionable. Clearly he was most himself when speaking with the second of poetry's Three Voices, that which Mr. Eliot has defined as that heard in 'poetry intended to amuse or instruct, poetry that tells a story, poetry that preaches or points a moral'; indeed one of Bjørnson's poems called 'The Poet' explicitly describes his office as that of a 'weekday preacher', as one who speaks as a prophet, who rallies and sustains his people, chastises their sins, takes up arms against cowardice and ignorance and acts as the champion of women, of the weak and of all who suffer. The pattern of communication on which these poems are constructed is for the most part that of one speaking to many, not so much a quiet button-holing but as an open exhortation, expressed not in a confidential manner but in a ringing tone, and spoken not 'under four eyes' but as the cynosure of a thousand. Their peculiar power lies in the directness and forcefulness of their altruism, in the simple and moving enunciation of the homelier emotions; they are moreover supremely singable, and this, along with their strongly patriotic appeal, took them deep into the national consciousness.

And no doubt it is here that one can see some reason for Bjørnson's comparative lack of appeal to an English-speaking public so ready to acclaim his contemporary, Henrik Ibsen: namely that this public is made up of detached bystanders who have never been compounded into a responsive audience; belonging to a different national tradition, it is insulated against his spell. In his works he reached on occasion heights of sublimity unapproached by any other Norwegian writing in his century, Ibsen not excluded; but taken all together, the whole corpus of his writing is too often and too deeply riven by serious flaws of taste, of artistry, of structural design—flaws for which the fervour of his enthusiasms and the vigour of his denunciations do not wholly compensate. Great though his stature may be as a figure in world literature, to Norway he meant infinitely more as a noble and generous and eloquent spokesman; and an outsider's view of his works sees them more as permanent reminders of brilliance than as living proofs of it.

★ 7 ★

ALEXANDER KIELLAND

A man cannot be a heretic, it has been said, except by starting from some inherited orthodoxy; the inheritance of Alexander Kielland included a grandfather who was said to have been the richest man in Norway in his day, a family tradition of true-blue conservatism, a childhood that still had an element of old-world charm in its patterns of living, and an education that was a protracted enjoinder to 'fear God and honour the King'; by his heresies against the twin dictates of heredity and environment, he emerged as one of the most extreme radical writers Norway has ever known.

He came riding on the crest of a wave at a time when Norwegian literature was at flood tide. The first six years of his literary career, from 1879 to 1884, saw the publication of Ibsen's *A Doll's House, Ghosts, An Enemy of the People* and *The Wild Duck*, of Bjørnson's *Leonarda, The New System, A Gauntlet, Beyond Our Power* and *The Heritage of the Kurts*, and of Jonas Lie's *Rutland, Go Ahead!, One of Life's Slaves* and *The Family at Gilje*; Kielland's own fluent and uninhibited contribution to these six astonishing years included six novels, three collections of short stories and a volume of plays. Although his reputation is that of novelist, the first work he wrote was in fact a play, *Homewards* (*Paa Hjemveien*), which was printed in the periodical *Nyt norsk tidsskrift* in the summer of 1878; his first book, published through the good offices of Bjørnson (whom he met in Paris), was of short stories (*Novelletter*) and it appeared appropriately enough on Labour Day, 1879; with their quiet wit and their elegance of style, they made an immediate impact. His first novel was begun on the encouragement of Georg Brandes, who urged him to try the longer narrative form since (he said) neither Ibsen nor Bjørnson seemed capable of producing a proper novel; it was completed within a few months and published in the spring of 1880 with the title *Garman and Worse* (*Garman & Worse*). Two more books, a collection of short stories and a volume of plays followed in the autumn of the same year; then in the spring of 1881, his second and much more sharply polemic novel *Workers* (*Arbeidsfolk*) appeared, to be followed later in the same year by *Else*. 1882 brought the publication of *Skipper Worse*, a novel which deals with the earlier history of the Stavanger firm of Garman and Worse at the time of the religious movement called Haugianism; and also the *Two short stories from Denmark* (*To novelletter fra Danmark*). *Poison* (*Gift*), a novel on the theme of education, appeared in 1883, with its sequel *Fortuna* in 1884. In 1884, however—a year of significant left-wing victories in Norwegian politics—it was as though the wave broke; for a time it continued under its own impetus, but without the same surging buoyancy; by 1891 it was altogether spent. Two shorter narrative works, *Snow* (*Sne*, 1886) and *Midsummer Festival* (*Sankt Hans Fest*, 1887), and three plays, *Three Couples* (*Tre par*, 1886), *Betty's Guardian* (*Betty's formynder*, 1887) and *The Professor* (*Professoren*, 1888) belong to the later period of his authorship; his last novel *Jacob* came in the year 1891, after which he abandoned creative writing altogether; in 1905 however, a few months before his death, he published a short work on Napoleon, which still contrived to be more a kind of social polemic than history.

The bulk of Kielland's work takes as its setting his native town of Stavanger, yet the regionalism of it is no narrow thing; and Ibsen deceived himself when he complained (if indeed he was correctly reported) that Kielland had only one topic, and that soon exhausted. Especially would it be a mistake to ignore the breadth of European thought that sustains both the themes of the novels and their urbane style. England, France and Germany, as well as his native Scandinavia, played a formative part in shaping his artistry: he devoured the works of John Stuart Mill—'You must read the *whole* of Stuart Mill', he counselled his sister in 1880—studied Darwin and read Dickens with much enjoyment; France it was that beckoned when he first seriously began to consider a writer's career, and when Brandes criticized *Workers* for being too 'English' in quality, Kielland replied that he 'would ten times rather bear French arms'; in Heine, he admired the scornful renunciation of 'the grand gesture', and in later life he admitted: 'I admire him in a way and to a degree I have never confessed to anybody—I think from a kind of jealousy'; whilst from the writings of Kierkegaard and Strindberg and from the personal encouragement of Georg Brandes he drew immense profit. His vision in the novels is carefully and even narrowly focused, but the things it registered were noted and pondered by a mind nourished by wide reading and by careful study of the European scene.

Once he had stationed himself within this restricted milieu, his natural inclination was then to take a panoramic view; the perspective in the earliest novels, *Garman and Worse* and *Workers*, is that of a wide-angled lens that sweeps over a whole range of characters, creating a group portrait in which the separate figures show their individuality not as independent beings so much as members of a household, of a family, of a parish; this was the method, he thought, that best served his purposes of social reform. The wealth of minor characterization in them has evoked the description 'Dickensian', whilst Brandes thought that *Workers* reminded him of Thackeray, and urged its author to apply himself rather to Flaubert as a model; in particular he advised him to limit the number of persons, to try to present a few characters in their totality, to offer a more profound analysis of them, 'to show them in profile, in half-profile and full-face, in all situations'. The fruits of this advice are best seen in the two novels *Poison* and *Fortuna*, where Kielland's psychological analysis of the hero Abraham Løvdahl (i.e. Kielland's own 'unhappy Doppelgänger') was firm and assured.

His novels were rooted, as he himself asserted, deep in a sense of indignation—indignation at the deceits of public life, at the hypocrisies of the Church, at the ruthlessness of reaction, at the duplicity of capitalism. *Workers* took as its target the corruption and inefficiency of Government officials, *Else* the smug self-satisfaction of the well-to-do, *Poison* the stuffiness of grammar school education, *Fortuna* the morality of big business, *Snow* the bigotry of the Church, *Midsummer Festival* the presumption of those who 'think they have God in their pockets', *Jacob* the dishonesties of public life. And yet there is about these fierce spasms of disgust and about the forms they took in his work something rather larger than life, something a little too assertive, something willed; and it is perhaps significant that the thing that roused him to a more natural fury than anything else was the suggestion that his indignation was a pose, was not wholly genuine; when one of the critics dismissed his radicalism as something that did not really go very deep, Kielland wrote to his brother-in-law: 'What I feel like trouncing him for is . . . his tirelessly assuring people that all this Kielland business is only good-natured fun; that, of course, Herr Kielland pretends he is serious about his view of life, but only because he knows it is modern; Herr Kielland is in reality a harmless bonvivant, the public must not allow itself to be misled.' His radicalism was of course no base deception, nor was it even innocent self-deception; but it was the product of a sensitive and extraordinarily active conscience which, together with a ready will, drove him to adopt emotional attitudes that were not strictly felt in any comparable degree. One notes the apologetic terms of his letter to Bjørnson where he complains that his first novel showed a tendency to become too 'humorous' and that he could not inject 'the proper evil' into it; and after it was completed, he regretted that it was too tame, that it had not become what it should have been because he had been too timid. Throughout the earlier years of his authorship he was, as his letters reveal, constantly urging himself on to extremes of radicalism, making a virtue of ferocity, and turning a natural propensity into a thing of determined resolution: 'He who wants to rouse people,' he wrote, 'must exaggerate. . . . Certainly I have exaggerated, I did it consciously.' Even Brandes at one point— to Kielland's hurt surprise—thought he had overdone his censure; and Bjørnson also sensed some unnaturalness, even though he ascribed it to the wrong reasons of self-advertisement, and in writing of one of the novels, said: 'You have, by your desire to demonstrate what a hell of a fellow Alexander Kielland is, exploded nearly every situation.'

Indeed, perhaps the most remarkable thing about Kielland's life and work was that the slightest occasion for self-reproach or self-criticism constituted for him an irresistible challenge; let him once become aware in himself of any moral or artistic weakness, any vulnerability to criticism from himself or others, and his will responded at once not merely to repair the implied fault but to transform weakness into strength, not merely to vacate the untenable position but to withdraw in order to assault it. 'The force that drives me and puts heat into my words,' he wrote, 'is a bad conscience, the knowledge that I am so well off.' After completing his legal studies, marrying at twenty-three and apparently settling down to a life of managing a brickworks, he ruefully discovered that all he was fit for was 'to tell jokes, play the flute and fish for salmon'; the consequence was that in 1873 he quietly left his home town for Paris to devote himself to writing. When a self-analysis of his powers seemed to tell him that he lacked imagination, that he seemed more likely to succeed in the role of moral philosopher than in that of imaginative writer, he met the challenge with such *élan* that by his achievement he ranked himself along with Ibsen, Bjørnson and Lie as one of Norway's 'big four', distinguished especially by his elegance and nimbleness of style. He constantly rebuked himself on the score of laziness, and on one occasion he implored Brandes to give him 'a kick in the pants' to cure him of it—yet within twelve years he wrote no less than nine novels, three collections of short stories and a number of plays, together with a wealth of correspondence that, in the opinion of many, marks the highest point of his whole achievement. He accused himself of moral cowardice and yet performed prodigies of literary courage; he learnt to tame his impetuosity, to develop the oblique approach by hint and implication, to adopt the technique of withholding the key-word 'so that the reader himself found the word on his lips without your having had to give it to him', to conceal the message so that it lies like the charge in a bomb 'that explodes only when it has struck'. Regretting his inability to construct a

novel, he adopted the technique of writing the final chapters of
the works first, so that they all have at least a clearly defined
direction even though they are not always wholly admirable in
their shape. And finally, after a decade of fulminating against the
tenants of public office, after years of expressing the artist's scorn
of the official, he suddenly and dramatically abandoned literature
and accepted the appointment of Mayor of Stavanger, and later
that of Sheriff of Romsdal.

Just as the facts contradict, or were made to contradict, his
self-reproaches on the score of unimaginativeness, timidity and
laziness, so one must regard with some suspicion those other
equally treacherous statements of self-congratulation; in particular one must take at something more than its face value that
statement of his which is most commonly associated with his
work: 'It is my pride to be an honest adherent of utilitarian
poetry, and you must also come down to this in the end if you
want to write anything about me.' There is in this statement the
same air of willed defiance, the same challenging aggressiveness
that marked his whole career; and it invites the suspicion that
whilst it may be true, it may not be the whole truth. However
much he may have tried to persuade himself that his characters
lacked subtlety of light and shade—'I light a bonfire in the
middle, as it were, in which I want to burn some social evil or
other; and round this are grouped a flock of characters, upon
whom the gleams of the fire fall more or less strongly, but always
only with illumination from the fire'—nevertheless he reckoned
without the involuntary betrayal of self that accompanies all
writing in some degree or other. However much he delighted in
embracing the moralist's view of things, or prided himself on his
practical aims, the element of exploration in his work always
dominated that of mere exposure. These novels never lie in a
single plane, whether one calls that plane 'utilitarianism' or anything else; they were punitive in a double sense, were both social
criticism and self-criticism at the same time, criticism if not
always of what he was, then at least of what he had escaped
becoming, or of what he and those near him had stood for; they
are a demonstration of the truth that John Stuart Mill formulated

when he stated in his *Logic* that 'all phenomena of society are phenomena of human nature'. It has, for example, not escaped attention that his social rebels are all weak, and that their fathers (or those in *loco parentis*), invested as they are with society's authority, stand for all that their sons seek to combat; much of this is a quite unambiguous reflection of Kielland's own relations with his father. But then Kielland had two 'fathers', his natural father and his 'father confessor' Georg Brandes, one representing an older, patrician order, and the other a newer and more problematical, but each in his own way the object of Kielland's ambivalent attention. There is in this something that makes his seemingly straightforward 'problem literature' a thing of unexpected and often unsuspected depth.

Conscience and will tempered all Kielland's decisions, self-reproach and application refined his style; but his career enacted a kind of enantiodromia, a 'turning of each thing into its opposite' that was partly willed and partly intuitive. Beneath it all there is this substratum of ambivalence: a hate that is not without its admixture of admiration, an indignation tinged with sympathy, and alongside the barbed irony another irony of a subtler kind that says one thing and hints only at another, something of which Kielland himself might well have been unconscious.

⋆ 8 ⋆

JONAS LIE

Those qualities that made Lie immediately popular in the 'seventies and 'eighties have little to do with his real and considerable merit. He was hailed as an author in whose work many ordinary people were able to recognize if not themselves then at least their neighbours; his novels were welcomed because they did for fisher folk what Bjørnson had done for those who worked the land—treated these classes for the first time in Norway as subjects fit for serious literary consideration. His popularity was that of a great innovator, the first author to write of Nordland for over 150 years, the man who wrote the first novels of the sea, the first novels of commercial life, the first love novels even, of modern Norway. But it is not among such accidents of history that one seeks for reasons why Lie has worn so well; the solider virtues that give his work intrinsic worth in addition to their historical importance are to be sought elsewhere. In the same way, and for much the same reasons, a new appraisal of the respective merits of the separate novels is about due. A contemporary public that for twenty years had given its support to Lie, and in so doing had formed certain expectations in respect of his authorship, was disinclined to welcome those darker and less comfortable works that came from his pen after 1890. It still belongs to the orthodox view to think of Lie in terms of the admittedly brilliant but sober realism of *Go Ahead!* and *The Family at Gilje* than to appreciate at their true value the more complex and difficult virtues of, say, *Dyre Rein* or of *When the Iron Curtain falls*. Popular esteem and critical evaluation are still to some extent confusedly intertwined.

It took a crippling bankruptcy to turn him from a dilettante

7

poet into a novelist of the first rank. Nothing seemed on the face
of things less propitious than that a one-time successful and even
wealthy lawyer, approaching middle-age, should take to writing
fiction with the immediate aim of making enough money to pay
back his creditors; time showed, however, that this was less important as a motive than it was a mechanism of release, something which, when allied with the encouragement he received
from his friend Bjørnson and from his wife Thomasine, helped
him to overcome an inhibiting lack of confidence and so find his
true vocation. The events of his early manhood, his legal training, his ten years of practice in the law, together with his comparatively late début as a writer—he was thirty-seven when his
first novel *The Visionary* (*Den fremsynte*) appeared in 1870,
although he had published a small volume of poems four years
earlier—were not without some (and probably on the whole
beneficial) influence on his style. Detachment, precision, careful
attention to significant detail, virtues that one associates with the
legal mind, along with a sense of assurance and balance that go
with greater maturity of development, all these are present in his
prose; such are the qualities that prompted Brandes to call him
Norway's most 'amiable' author, and allowed Arne Garborg to
write:

As a poet, Lie is of a positive and harmonious nature. He has left
behind the time of youth, of cloudy fermentation and of immature and
incomplete view of life; he is a man with a healthy intellectual life, and
one can clearly see from his writing that he has finished his inner
development and has found a standpoint and poise. No wild, stumbling
haste, no disharmonies, no striving for effect, no thoughtless fluttering
and straying in the void—everything is natural, assured, rounded.

But these virtues can never in themselves be a source of
creative imagination, only the means of controlling and disciplining it; and the real source of Lie's narrative power, that which
provided the sap for what otherwise would have been dry and
brittle, lay much deeper: a chthonic fantasy, which Lie attributed
in part to the presence of gipsy blood in his veins but which had
also surely been stimulated and developed by his childhood years

in Nordland. As the Border country was to Scott, as Wessex was to Thomas Hardy, so the Nordland was to Lie, an indispensable ingredient in the chemistry of the authorship of this 'true-hearted but grotesque old argufier', as an English scholar has called him. It was not merely that he was able in later years to tap his store of experiences, or to refresh early memories by revisiting this mystery-ridden land of the midnight sun whither he had gone at the age of five and where he had spent seven of his most impressionable years; not merely that he was able to write about Nordland, a region which ever since the time of Petter Dass had lacked a pen to give literary expression to it, but rather that his whole attitude to life was coloured and his personal sense of the human scene developed by his years there. Years later, in his novel *Evil Powers* (*Onde magter*, 1890) he asked: 'Might there not be a little, exciting and incalculable troll concealed somewhere deep within', a remark that might well pass for self-analysis; for in spite of all the vigilance of his wife who stood sentry over his style, keeping out of his work much that was unworthy by her lights and maybe also much that was worthy by ours—in spite of all this, the troll that inhabited Lie's fantasy is always there in his work as a presence; and on the one occasion when it seemed itself to take command, in the collection of *Weird Tales* (*Trold*, 1891-2) the result was something quite unique and personal. One agrees rather more readily therefore with Garborg's other description of Lie as an 'eruptive' nature, one that found delight in the mysterious and irrational; this was something immediately apparent in *The Visionary*, incontestable in *Weird Tales*, and which informed the greater part of his work after 1890, a quality that lies at the very centre of his work, however much the staider realism of some of his other and often more highly esteemed novels seem to belie it.

There is no knowing how immature, how uneven his first novel, *The Visionary*, was in its original form, for his wife cut away the half of it before it was sent for Bjørnson's scrutiny and opinion; even as it stands, it is fumblingly and self-consciously organized. But its qualities of genuine vitality and freshness of vision are at once evident, even though only intermittently so, and there is no doubt that for such reasons alone it ranks high among Lie's novels. Structurally, it is too elaborate for its touchingly simple theme of the love of a mentally unstable boy, gifted with second sight, for his childhood sweetheart; it is a novice's eagerness that attempts to incorporate within its eighty pages or so a fictional narrator who disappears after the first section, two separate sets of posthumous papers, some flash-back reminiscences, a digression on the character of Nordland and its inhabitants, and a number of interpolated folk tales. The manner of address is on occasion distressingly arch: 'I gave myself up to my memories,' says the fictional narrator whilst his childhood friend, newly met after many years, is out of the room, 'which I will report here, even at the danger that the reader might suppose my friend is staying out rather a long time preparing the punch.' Nor is there, except for the hero's bare assertion at the end of his story that Susanne's love for him has saved his sanity, any real justification for Lie's claiming the point of the story to be that of showing 'love's power of healing the sick mind'. There is magic in this book, but it is in the creation of atmosphere and not in the organization of its parts.

By contrast, the novels that immediately followed seem almost too well architected, their complicated outlines flowing almost too smoothly; and with the disappearance of the earlier crudeness there went also much of the poetic urgency. It is in these novels, especially *The Barque 'Future'* (*Tremasteren 'Fremtiden'*, 1872) and *The Pilot and his Wife* (*Lodsen og hans hustru*, 1874) that Lie developed his eye for detail, his sense of the insinuative effect of highly-charged triviality that has caused some to call his realism 'impressionistic' and which reaches perfection in such novels as *Rutland* (1880), *Go Ahead!* (*Gaa paa!*, 1882) and *The Family at Gilje* (*Familjen paa Gilje*, 1883). These novels are the work of inspired craftsmanship, but not of intuitive artistry; for all their brilliance, it is as though their author's naturally wayward imagination is too tightly reined. When he writes in this vein, his novels often seem to commend themselves as exercises in description and portraiture, an impression that much of his sub-titling—'Pictures from Nordland', 'Life up north', 'An

Interior from the Forties'—often seems to reinforce: nor does one forget that a good deal of his popularity as a novelist derived from his skill as a seascape artist. But one realizes nevertheless that the descriptions have always been set to work: 'The reader must be brought to understand the peculiar mental composition of the hero,' he wrote; 'it is towards this that the various pictures serve.'

He attempted, and in part succeeded, in holding himself aloof during these years from the tempestuous social debates of the age, in spite of attempts to play him off as a conservative force against the strident radicalism of Bjørnson. He was of all his contemporaries the least programmatical, and sought isolation by deliberate choice: 'In our restless agitated age, you can as a poet do one of two things: *either* enter into politics with your lyre . . . in the fashion of Wergeland, *or* isolate yourself to get peace so as to live for and in one's work, that it might become something worth while.' It was partly this view of the poet's responsibility, partly his reluctance to live in a land where he still owed large sums of money, that led him to live for over twenty-eight years abroad, in Paris, in Germany and in Italy. But he was still unable to prevent a good deal of social comment and a large number of 'problems' from finding their way into his novels: in some more or less directly, although with a lack of overt partisanship most untypical of his epoch, such as the problem of the illegitimate child in *One of Life's Slaves* (*Livsslaven*, 1883), the struggles of the poor seamstress in *Maisa Jons* (1888), or the question of the social status of women in *The Family at Gilje* and *The Commodore's Daughters* (*Kommandørens døtre*, 1886); or sometimes so obliquely that his criticisms require a quite sophisticated interpretation, as with his disguised strictures on the stagnation of Norway in *Go Ahead!* But it is a leading characteristic of his art to show detachment; Kielland was so disappointed when the author of *The Family at Gilje* failed to pursue and expose 'the gluttonous, guzzling officials as the fathers of the present ones', that he dismissed it as 'a charming novel about nothing': he could not see that such a course would have run altogether contrary to Lie's view of literature.

With the publication of *Evil Powers* in 1890, a distinct change is visible in Lie's view of the things that had hitherto made up his narrative world. 'I had begun to *see* people in earnest,' he wrote to a friend, '. . . previously I had taken them for what they gave themselves out to be. I knew well enough that there was envy in the world and avarice and the like, but it was something terribly nasty and far away; but then I saw that it is quite close. I saw envy cross my own threshold, knew that it is to be found in the best, in me, in you, in everyone.' *Evil Powers*, which was in part a reproach to Bjørnson with whom he had lately quarrelled, was the first raw and unprocessed expression of this new realization; the *Weird Tales* took over this same idea of the presence of secret, uncontrollable forces within the individual mind and, using the mould of the folk-tale, made of the idea an aesthetically distanced and consummate work of art; whilst *Dyre Rein* (1896), by treating the hero's awareness of the presence of these forces within himself and tracing the personal tragedy that follows from this awareness, added a whole new dimension. It was left to one of Lie's last and most powerful novels *When the Iron Curtain Falls* (*Naar Jernteppet falder*, 1901) to stress the cathartic and therapeutic value of having withstood the impact of these inner forces and won through. A group of passengers on an Atlantic steamer suddenly hears in mid-ocean that an infernal machine planted in the ship will blow them up within the hour; in such circumstances, which stand as a kind of shorthand definition for any serious crisis that life might present to the individual, each person shows his self-control or lack of it; and when it is later discovered that the whole thing has been a false alarm, the passengers see themselves and each other in a much clearer light.

Lie's name has often been coupled with that of Dickens, for whose work he is known to have had considerable regard; but it is rather with a writer like Stifter that he shows the closest affinity, both in the poetry of his realism and in the view of life that informs his work. In both of them, one finds as something central to their philosophy the notion of the destructive force of 'passion', in the sense of ungoverned emotion, and the threat that it exerts to the harmonious development of the individual; only when disciplined by experience and self-knowledge can it yield to a proper attitude of resignation. 'We all have a tiger-like temperament', said Stifter; he also insisted that 'passion is always immoral'. One finds the same kind of imagery in a remark Lie made in 1880: 'It is a part of my observation of life—this discrepancy between intellectual development and moral ignorance that can manifest itself in one and the same person. Passion, this wild beast within man, breaks out the moment he least expects it; for he is not practised in controlling it.' The moral development towards peace and understanding is one that in one form or another characterizes the life of many of Lie's creations, from David Holst in *The Visionary* whose 'countenance had that transfigured look of a man who has wrestled with his fate and had now found peace and resignation', through Jon Zachariasen in *The Barque 'Future'* and Salve Kristiansen in *The Pilot and his Wife*, to the more sombre characters of the later works. To win the moral struggle, to emerge from the fires of passion cleansed and purged, is to achieve life's greatest victory.

★ 9 ★

SIGBJØRN OBSTFELDER

Sigbjørn Obstfelder's popular reputation in his native Norway
is a cloak that conceals rather than clothes him, a thing made
shapeless by anthologists and hagiographers acting with scant
regard for the true configuration of his poetry. It spreads over
the pages of the anthologies, in which a handful of poems
repetitively and monotonously create an image of their author as
one who—in the words of his best-known poem—had 'surely
come to the wrong planet'; and it is stretched in other ways by
those among his admirers who demand that the other dimensions
should be made to conform, who exaggerate his stature, inflate
his importance. Obstfelder was too modest a man and too modest
a poet to wear a garment so grotesquely misshapen. But in among
the catchwords and the cults, there nevertheless resides a talent
of a peculiarly fine but strangely limited distinction, a personality
for which to be stereotyped and to be deified are fates equally
disabling.

In spite of the attention Obstfelder has attracted in Scandinavia, there will be few in England or America who know his
name, fewer still his work; of his admittedly modest output of
published material—modest, that is, in comparison with the still
unpublished manuscript material which his editor claims would
fill a ten-volume variorum edition—only a selection of his lyrics
have so far been translated into English. In time, his work
belongs wholly to the eighteen-nineties: his first volume of poems
appeared in 1893, *A Cleric's Journal* (*En præsts dagbog*) posthumously in 1900, and to the years between there belong a
number of plays and dramatic fragments, including *The Red
Drops* (*De røde draaber*, 1897) and two one-act plays *In Spring*

(*Om vaaren*, 1898) and *Esther* (1899), several short prose works, among them the short novel *The Cross* (*Korset*, 1896), and a large number of fugitive pieces, sketches, articles, drafts and reminiscences, along with a group of works he called 'poems in prose'. Yet for all the sadness and the sense of unfulfilled promise that attaches to his early death, there seems in a way to be something grimly appropriate about the time and the manner of it, as though by his dying he had sought to add one final and almost ostentatious proof, to those he had already given by the pattern of his life, that his soul was in close rapport with the spirit of the *fin-de-siècle*. Of the characteristic figures of the period in England, it has been said that 'most of them died young, several were scarcely more than youths; some died of diseases which might have been checked or prevented in more careful lives; some were condemned to death at an early age by miserable maladies'. Born on 21 November 1866 as the seventh of sixteen children, compelled in 1891 to enter a mental asylum for some months to regain the balance of his mind, Obstfelder died of consumption at the age of thirty-three on 29 July 1900, the same year that witnessed the untimely deaths of Oscar Wilde and Ernest Dowson. It is almost as though his soul, like theirs, could not endure the passing of the decade. Even the last and characteristically macabre touch was not lacking; for on the same day that he was carried to his grave, his widow was delivered of their only child. It is not without good reason that, in addition to Rilke, four other writers are suspected of having used Obstfelder as a model on which to form some character typical of the age.

Here and there outside Scandinavia, the name of Obstfelder may be recognized as that of the young man on whom Rilke modelled the diarist hero of *Die Aufzeichnungen des Malte Laurids Brigge*. The recognition tends to have two unfortunate consequences: in the first place, it prompts comparisons not only in style but in value between Rilke and Obstfelder, an undertaking that greatly flatters the latter, for the two poets are by any notation of values barely comparable; it has also led some into accepting *A Cleric's Journal* itself as a source for *Malte Laurids Brigge*, which seems hardly justified on the evidence. The most that seems justified is to find in their common ancestry the name of Kierkegaard. It is true that Rilke was acquainted with some of Obstfelder's work before *Malte Laurids Brigge* was written; his correspondence of these years contains occasional mention of the Norwegian, and on 4 December 1904 he sent as a gift to Lou Andreas-Salomé some unspecified book by Obstfelder, saying 'Ein kleines Buch von Obstfelder sende ich Dir, darin das und jenes mir lieb geworden ist'; and he later described Obstfelder as 'a poet of subtle impressionism and intense sensibility'. But it is rather the details of Obstfelder's life and personality—which Rilke might well have learned from Ellen Key, at different times the confidante of both men—that provided material for *Malte Laurids Brigge*; Obstfelder was an example of the *Früheentrückten*, of those who died young; for as Rilke later told his French translator Maurice Betz, two things had struck him about Obstfelder—that he too had lived as a Scandinavian in Paris, and that he had died at the age of thirty-three, without having given his work the full measure of his tormented and generous soul. He stands then, as Professor E. M. Butler has suggested, to *Malte Laurids Brigge* as Jerusalem stood to Werther: 'The suicide of Jerusalem, and the death of the young Norwegian Sigbjørn Obstfelder, provided the two high priests of poetry with the . . . victim, whose blood had to drench the altar.'

The torment of soul that Rilke remarked in Obstfelder is conspicuous as the most obvious characteristic in his life and work, and particularly so in *A Cleric's Journal*; yet it determined his career and coloured his poetry not so much by the nature of the elements of which it was compounded, nor even by the intensity with which it manifested itself, as by Obstfelder's own awareness of and insight into it. The strife in his mind was a personal variant of the conventional *fin-de-siècle* malady of the conflicting claims of life and art: and in his case it took the form of how to resolve the individual's worth as a solitary, independent, creative spirit, questioning, brooding, uncertain, with the same individual's potentialities as an element in the social pattern, confident and purposeful. As he wrote in 1894: 'It is only when one sees the great cities, the beating hearts of the age, that one experiences the urge to feel oneself *at one* with this working, suffering and sinning society of men, to understand what it does and what it leaves undone, to share sickness with the sick, and to understand it that one might be able to heal.' Mystic by nature, materialist by conscience, he found the problem of how to hold the balance between the two obsessive, something both to brood upon and also by his own career to enact: and whenever it seemed any one side in the struggle was gaining ascendency, he trimmed the balance by some prodigious exertion of will. The tenacity with which he carried out decisions once taken was paradoxically sustained by the very knowledge of his own native irresolution: 'Moodiness [*tungsindet*]—this word which I have pronounced so many times—undermines me and my will. And when it is not moodiness, then it is irresolution. I set myself objectives, I draw up lists in my tormented brain, but all that happens is that not a single heading on my lists is ever accomplished—as the result of my sinking into brooding about it.' His letters bear witness to the variety of plans he toyed with and the rapidity with which he switched his restless attention from one scheme to another—one of which, incidentally, was to learn English well enough to become Walt Whitman's successor. But always the main tension (with him, as with the fictional diarist of *A Cleric's Journal*) was that between what lies within the individual and what exists without, between solitary contemplation and social action. By his determination to implicate himself in life, by attempting to discipline what could be disciplined only at fearful cost, he kept at high tension the torment in his soul, driving himself to the point where his reason temporarily collapsed, and even ultimately to his death.

A rough graph of his life's history shows the violence of the fluctuations to which this conflict of nature and will subjected him. Even as a child he had shown considerable imaginative talent, and when he was of an age to enter the university, he enrolled as a student of philology, leaving himself also free to pursue his interests in music, literature and philosophy—it is no surprise, in the light of certain passages in *A Cleric's Journal*, to discover that Kierkegaard occupied him greatly at this time. But

then in 1888 there came one of those decisions that social conscience, will-power and an urge to be out in the wide world all
seemed to combine to force upon him: he abandoned his
linguistic studies in favour of engineering, something that would
permit him to make some practical and material contribution to
society and would also ease his chances of emigrating. After two
years at a technical school, he went to America to join his younger
brother in the late summer of 1890. But his life in America—in
Milwaukee at first, and later in Washington Heights and Chicago
—was one of disappointment and frustration, and almost at once
the deeper forces in his nature began to assert themselves; he
determined to return home, this time obeying the decision to
devote himself to what is probably the least practical of all the
arts: music. He arrived back in Norway in 1891, weary, dispirited,
and almost at once suffered mental collapse. Later the old conflicts merely took new form; he embarked on a literary career,
but alongside his poetry he felt the need to participate in the
social debates of the age; he wrote many articles on the contro-
versial questions of the day, on temperance, on the social status
of women, on architecture. His restless spirit drove him to lead
a wandering, rootless existence which, as some of his letters show,
was painfully at variance with a deep-seated desire to marry and
settle down to a life of quiet, purposeful endeavour. Copenhagen
and Paris, Stockholm, Berlin, Amsterdam, Prague and London
saw him for brief periods, his travels often being undertaken
slowly and painfully on foot; eventually he did marry, but his
death followed only two years later.

What distinguishes him from the majority of his European
contemporaries in art and literature is, however, not so much that
the fluctuations of his soul were more violent, nor that the decisions in terms of daily conduct were more extreme, but that he was
fin-de-siècle not as the result of self-indulgence but rather as the
consequence of vain self-discipline. It is not often that one finds,
in his articles or his correspondence, any hint that he felt himself
in any way set apart from his fellows; but where phrases of this
nature do occur, they suggest that he felt himself distinguished
from others not by any greater sensitivity or more intense

emotional life but by the measures he adopted to control and discipline himself. It cannot be denied that there was a strong streak of eroticism in his temperament; yet in 1887 he wrote on the question of sexual restraint among young men, priding himself on the fact that he was 'one of the few who have really striven to be worthy of Woman in this respect'. And he used similar phrases about his literary composition, claiming distinction not for his sensibility but for his strength of purpose, asserting that there was surely scarcely any other young author who had the strength of will *he* had to hold fast to a composition for years. Where others had seen their sensibility as a thing to be carefully fostered and nurtured, he saw it as a threat to the living of a full life, as something inimical to active participation in human affairs; where others sought to escape from actuality into a world of vivid and possibly ·exotic sensation, he knew that such an escape was only too fatally easy for one of his nature, and unceasingly sought to resist. There was no thrill in giving himself up to the ecstasy of the moment, but only a sense of betrayal and guilt; there was nothing in him of the *poseur*, for he feared rather than exploited the mystic strain in his make-up and lamented his inability to share in the material triumphs of honest labour. He was too painfully aware of what Walt Whitman had called 'the hiatus in singular eminence', that sense of lack that possesses the poet when he feels he is too remote from common life, felt it perhaps even more acutely than Whitman who had not, as Obstfelder had, experienced the real impact of the machine on society. Engagement, not detachment, was what he asked from life.

The percipience that was his, he therefore employed not as a medium through which to experience ever more vivid and unusual sensation, but as an instrument to aid him in his quest for meaning in the universe. 'I believe,' he wrote to a friend in 1895, the year he began work on *A Cleric's Journal*, 'that I have, as scarcely any other young author has, the urge to penetrate into the mystery of nature, to see Man in the light of what is eternal in time, space and energy, to see the changing forms of life, flower, larva, infusoria in great array as the song of Universal

Life'. Portentous though these phrases may sound when thus lifted out of their context in Obstfelder's life and art, it would nevertheless be false to think of him as an over-earnest and solemnly intense young man, destitute of all humour; it is true that he took himself seriously, true also that he showed no inhibitions about asking the big questions; but it is equally obvious from other evidence that he could on occasion write with much wit, and that satire came naturally to him. Indeed one wonders whether his refusal to indulge in this satirical form was not perhaps another piece of self-discipline, another act of controlled suppression in respect of something that he felt unworthy of a conscientious poet, something that was too often the refuge of those who were not wholly certain whether they were serious about things or not. Poets, he says in one of his shorter articles, are like those who lend us lenses, telescopes, microscopes, the better to see and comprehend what is all around us. His sensibility was thus put out to work, becoming a device for attempting to trace and record the connections between things, connections too tenuous and too fine for the coarser and less sensitive minds of his fellows to catch.

All this is clearly mirrored in *A Cleric's Journal*, that work which occupied him during the last years of his life. Rilke's summary of it—'the story of a soul who, in his despairing attempts to approach God, actually becomes more estranged from Him, a prey to an intellectual fever that brings him to despair'—is only true in part. A good deal of the book admittedly grew out of the mental turmoil that had accompanied his breakdown, and it is not without relevance that Obstfelder requested that certain letters written to his brother from the asylum should be returned to him. Moreover he tended, after this time, to see the problems of existence more and more as religious problems; and in *A Cleric's Journal* the application of a religious framework to those ideas which habitually preoccupied him is immediately evident. But the mysticism is only one aspect, just as the problem of practical living is another, of something much more crucial: the purpose of life itself, the search for some kind of certainty in this uncertain world, whether it concerns the nature of God or the patterns of community living. The bishop, the doctor and the worker all have, in this journal, their own kind of certainty, their own confident belief in some chosen faith, dogmatic, socialist, materialist, as the case may be; only the lonely poet has doubts and the compulsion to express them. It is a book with the courage of its lack of convictions.

Some have seen in Obstfelder's work an attempt to do with language what his great contemporary Edvard Munch tried to do with paint; and the judgement Obstfelder himself passed on Munch might be regarded as applying with almost equal validity to his own work. He stresses the fact that Munch was a receptive artist, whose greatness lay in the subtlety of his colour and not in any power of reshaping or manipulating the forms he saw in life; his talent did not run to the creation of new lines:

But those lines that *are* [wrote Obstfelder], those he sees as no other man. And it is as if, from all that exists, from all existence with all its forms and all its chaos, he extracts *one* line which he constantly worked towards and which he endeavours to turn more and more beautifully. Is it the line of his inmost Self? Or is it the one drawn by the encounter between his soul's plan and that of the universe about him?

This surely applies equally to *A Cleric's Journal*; the course it follows—and would have pursued further if time and health had permitted—is that traced by the encounter between Obstfelder's tormented soul and cosmic reality. What he was not endowed with was the ability to project his experiences, to give them the newly moulded form of poetic invention, to organize, to construct; instead he had the capacity for marvel, for standing and looking and listening and dreaming. In this work, he does not set out to create a poetic world complete with his own inner and inherent laws, but instead endeavours, with the utmost delicacy, to follow the twists and turns, the evasions, the withdrawals and the probings of a soul's progress in an exploration of this world.

To call his work symbolist, as is often done, is therefore true only in a very limited sense; visionary is rather the term that more exactly describes his idiosyncratic attempts to say the unsayable—'those feelings,' as he wrote in his early student days, 'that have not acquired the form of thought'. Whereas Rilke, for example, built up a range of symbols (the angel, the puppet, the acrobat) to assist him in saying *das Unsägliche*, Obstfelder found that what he had similarly called *det usigelige* communicated itself in visions. Time and again in *A Cleric's Journal*, the sense of the mysterious oneness that fills the universe is translated into purely visual terms, into the things that a mystically endowed man might see: patterns, networks, nearly visible threads that link the things of life, these are the images that keep recurring; even music which meant so much to him and for which he showed so sensitive an understanding, is a thing to be watched, even rhythm is a little triangle or square drawn by the conductor's hand that wings out over the massed instruments of the orchestra. This prepotently visual sense, it is hinted, makes difficulties for a soul such as his: which is best able to contemplate and appreciate the ancient world when things stood still, when the universal design was a static and comprehensible thing, when the earth stood firm on its four corners; to trace a pattern in movement, to grasp the rhythm of things that are constantly changing, shifting position, rushing through space, that is something that makes demands on faculties other than the visual. For all Obstfelder's deep love and understanding of music, his imagination is one that feeds mainly on what the eye sees. This is possibly one of the reasons why, in spite of the studied simplicity of language, his prose has an ornamental quality, reminiscent of the earlier poetry of Stefan George who, as he himself implied, had to be content with a hot and decorative and bejewelled style because he was not mature enough to fashion it in a cool, metallic form, hard and smooth.

It is typical of Obstfelder that he should have oscillated between regarding *A Cleric's Journal* as his masterpiece and seeing it as a melancholy failure. At first it seemed like something momentous to him; in 1897, when he looked over what he had written, he felt that it was more profound than anything he had produced hitherto; and in the following year he was confirmed in this opinion—'the weightiest, the richest thing I have written'. But shortly before his death, he viewed it with complete despair: 'This book has come to be my misfortune. At one time I approached it with the greatest of expectations. . . . And more and more a deep despondency has possessed me. I have misgivings about what I have done. It does not seem to me to correspond to what I had in mind, nor to what I still feel I was capable of. . . . And of late I have been and am seized by the deepest disgust for this book.'

That the book in its present form is both unfinished and unrevised conditions to some extent one's valuation of it as a piece of literature. Where Rilke deliberately and for artistic reasons chose to leave *Malte Laurids Brigge* with its air of incompleteness, Obstfelder had no choice; not only does it lack its immediate concluding section—which Obstfelder had said would have taken a further three months' work—but even when thus completed, it was intended that it should serve only as the first section of a larger work. That it also lacks finish in another sense there is no need to dispute: some of its colours are crude, some of its extremely 'lyrical' passages distressingly self-conscious, and some of its lapses into exaltation disconcerting. But the world can now only take it as it was left: as a work of extreme honesty, full of the immediacy of experience, and remarkable as much by its delicacy and power of expression as by the resonance of its courage; as something, in other words, rather less than a masterpiece, rather more than a literary curiosity.

⋆ 10 ⋆

KNUT HAMSUN

The disabling thing is that there is no reliable English map of
the country. The few perfunctory reports we do have tell
of what seems to be an extensive tract of primitive, fictioneering
country, where life is lived stolidly and far from the abyss, where
farming offers a satisfying religion, where the going tests the
stamina rather than the agility, and all is dominated by a prize-
capped eminence called *Growth of the Soil*. Here, it is said, the
views are idyllic: 'If *Growth of the Soil* can be said to have any
plot at all—any story', wrote Katherine Mansfield guardedly, 'it
is the very ancient one of man's attempt to live in fellowship with
Nature.' An anonymous reviewer, writing not long ago of a
Hamsun novel newly translated, claimed: 'The kindest thing
one can say . . . is that it may appeal to the admirers of Mary
Webb.' And reading this, one feels one knows it all, or at least
enough: this is for addicts of simple wholesomeness, here you
get away from it all, back to the land in the service of the Good
Earth. And the modern reader, chary of naïve and emphatic
dogmas, trained on the dizzy slopes of meaningful ambiguity and
image cluster and archetypal pattern, and relishing a problem
for its awkwardness, turns hurriedly away from the prospect of
anything so ineluctably earthbound.

When Thomas Mann looked for parallels, however, he found
them rather in Dostoevski and Nietzsche.

I always loved him [he wrote of Hamsun in 1922], from my earliest
days. I early felt that neither Nietzsche nor Dostoevski had left behind in
their own countries a pupil of this rank. The incomparable charm of
his artistry captivated me as a 19 year old—and I shall never forget
what the novels *Hunger*, *Mysteries*, *Pan* and *Victoria* . . . once meant

to my susceptibilities. The world fame that fell to his name with the award of the Nobel Prize filled me with genuine personal satisfaction; never, I felt, had it fallen to one more worthy of it.

Nor was Mann the only one in these years to allow into his expressions of admiration phrases that made similar flattering comparisons. André Gide, whom Hamsun's first novel *Hunger* had taken by storm, referred to it in 1929 as a work of powerful originality; and in testifying to its profoundly personal and individual style, claimed that it was Dostoevskian in its execution with perhaps an even greater subtlety than in the work of the master himself. It had even happened that Hamsun in 1892 was publicly accused of laying Dostoevski under requisition, so strongly reminiscent was he of the great Russian.

In the quite grotesquely discrepant assessments—on this side of the Channel Hamsun as Mary Webb, and on the other Hamsun as Dostoevski—one could no doubt find the source of much easy entertainment, though perhaps not of a great deal of profit. Certainly, it was to Germany that Hamsun owed his wider European reputation, not to mention the greater part of his income: the literary acumen of Samuel Fischer helped to make of *Hunger* a Continental sensation; and with the appearance in the early 1890s of Hamsun's second novel *Mysteries*, there began the author's long association with the Munich publishing house of Albert Langen. In England, by contrast, it was not until thirty years after his début that Hamsun became generally known, when his Nobel Prize of 1920 was held by English publishers to constitute a kind of international certificate of competence; only two of his novels had appeared in English before this time: *Hunger* in 1899, and a slighter thing called *New Earth* in 1914, neither of them commercially successful or even esoterically influential. 'George Egerton' did her gushing best for him; she was his first translator, and her volume of short sketches entitled *Keynotes* carried a dedication in which the nature of her enthusiasm is surely and fatally betrayed: 'To Knut Hamsun, in memory of a day when the west wind and the rainbow met 1892–93.' One of the pieces in this collection, which seems to describe a visit to Hamsun, also brings in a cross-reference to

Nietzsche; but what a wealth of difference there is between Thomas Mann's measured deliberation and these girlish confidences: 'Did we not talk about anything? Of course we did. Tolstoi and his doctrine of celibacy. Ibsen's Hedda. Strindberg's view of the female animal. And we agreed that Nietzsche appealed to us immensely.' All Hamsun's novels (except *Editor Lynge*) are now translated into English; but our national attitude remains one of mutilating indifference.

This is a pity. And he who is deceived by the reports into setting out as for a clod-hopping, cross-country jaunt is soon in difficulty, on the jagged edges of the irony, on the shifting, ambiguous ground. Seemingly obvious routes peter out in bewildering thickets of psychological complexity, signposts are not to be trusted. A heavy freight of critical machinery, assembled with the idea of forcing a way through, is nothing but a liability in a terrain where progress is rather a matter of treading carefully.

Although *Hunger* burst upon the world of Scandinavian literature in 1890 with an explosive novelty, it was—as we can see more clearly today—merely the release in a new form of a body of thought that had been building up for the better part of a century; it was the expression in the literary mode of that same thing to which Freud was soon to give scientific formulation: speculation about the ways of the unconscious mind. It is natural to see the source of the tradition, if not the immediate and direct inspiration of these two men, in the work of Schopenhauer. The Hamsun biographies written by his wife and his son both bear witness to his fondness for referring them to Schopenhauer if they wished for true enlightenment about life and its ways; influence, of some kind and at some time, there must have been. The same cannot be said of Freud, however, who read Schopenhauer very late in life, although he was quick to acknowledge that Schopenhauer had been one of the forerunners of his own ideas, and he remarked on 'the far-reaching agreement between psycho-analysis and Schopenhauer's philosophy'. Both men, Hamsun and Freud, represent in their different ways a culmination of that interest in the ways of unconscious mental processes which might be said to have begun with Schelling, which had been systematically widened and deepened in the work of Schopenhauer and Carus and Eduard von Hartmann, and which was further exploited by the imaginative insight of Dostoevski, Nietzsche, and Strindberg.

No ponderous documentation is needed to prove what is obvious and what Hamsun himself freely admitted: that these three last-mentioned writers were in his early days of authorship the stars in his heaven. 'There is perhaps nobody who has been more influenced than I', he wrote in 1929. 'I am no man of stone, I am impressionable, excitable, hysterical some might think; perhaps I have learnt from all those authors I have read, how should I know! But in my younger days, none made such an impression on me as Dostoevski, Nietzsche and Strindberg.' Dostoevski, of whom Hamsun after completing *Hunger* read everything he could lay his hands on; Nietzsche, whose opinions the reader meets almost unmodified on nearly every page of *Mysteries*; and Strindberg, of whom Hamsun wrote in 1894: 'I always return to him again with joy; he has occupied me more than anybody else and taught me more than most.' His familiarity with the ideas of Hartmann, too, was considerable; as early as 1888 in Copenhagen he had discussed with friends and given unstinted praise to Hartmann's *Die Philosophie des Unbewussten*, praise so unqualified indeed that Georg Brandes was later moved to remark that Hamsun cherished 'a touching faith in Eduard von Hartmann's profundity'. Hamsun claimed to identify in Strindberg many of Hartmann's ideas transmuted into literature, for had not Strindberg himself acclaimed Hartmann as a thinker who had penetrated deep into the secrets of existence? One other name might be added to those whose psychological insight impressed Hamsun as worthy of emulation: Goncourt. Whether Hamsun, in the following passage written in 1890, intended some differentiation between the brothers or used the name collectively is not made explicit; but after discussing a likely theme and a likely character for narrative treatment, he wrote: 'I know only one psychological writer who could describe that character; not

Dostoevski, who makes even normal people abnormal, but Goncourt.'

To the early Hamsun, the issues were simple and unambiguous. The world of literature fell into two parts: the literature of external event and that of inner motive. Here was the social or 'problematical', there the psychological; the worthless and the valuable. To Marie Herzfeld, his German translator who had sent him a short work of her own composition, he wrote on 26 August 1890: 'I can see that your interests are also for the psychological, and that makes me really glad, for after all it is this alone that has the highest worth. Ordinary fiction about dances and engagements and excursions and marriages is nothing but reading for sea-captains and coachmen looking for an hour's entertainment. Cheap writing!' That it should also have seemed to his contemporaries as though, when making these distinctions, he also split the world into The Others and Me (plus perhaps Strindberg and Dostoevski) is a measure of the passion with which he put his views.

From January to October in 1891 he travelled through Norway on a lecture tour, the spice of which for his countrymen undoubtedly lay in the vigour with which he attacked the established great ones of Norwegian letters. One need not doubt that in attacking Ibsen—and attacking him to his face, for Ibsen attended his lectures in Kristiania—he knew he would help to distinguish himself not only from Ibsen but also *with* him in the public view; but even if one looks at his startling iconoclasm as a device, it is charitable to assume that it was a device to sell his ideas rather than to sell himself. The text of his lectures has unfortunately not been preserved, and practically all our information about them is derived from a number of press reports; but, as one might have foretold, his sharpest weapons were directed against those views of life that sought to represent Man as a wholly rational and explicable thing, and against those writers who, by the moralizing treatment of 'problems' in their works, imagined they could better their fellows and improve society by honest exhortation. 'Of the waking dreams, the mysterious feelings that emerge from the unconscious life of the mind, they

KNUT HAMSUN 119

know nothing', he is reported as having said; the proper role of literature had to be to 'pursue thought in its innermost concealed corners, on its darkest and most remote paths, in its most fantastic flights into mystery and madness, even to the distant spheres, to the gates of Heaven and Hell'.

The deeper attitude to literature and the novel in which these convictions were rooted can be defined with some precision by reference to two essays: 'Kristofer Janson' which appeared in 1888 but which had been written some time earlier; and 'From the Unconscious Life of the Mind' ('Fra det ubevidste Sjæleliv') which appeared in 1890. In the former, Hamsun makes a fundamental distinction from which many of his later ideas may be regarded as deriving: that between literature as 'popular education' and literature as 'art'. To address oneself to 'the people' (as Janson had done) instead of to the individual reader, to some empty abstraction instead of to a thinking, feeling, acting personality is to subordinate the artist to the preacher and debase the purpose of literature from that of 'striking home', of giving the reader the authentic thrill, to that of purveying commonplace practical wisdom and of trying to talk people out of their prejudices. It gives a picture of life with all its nagging complexities removed. Just as later, in his review of Bjørnson's *In God's Way* in 1890, he objected to the excessive injections of 'improving' instruction, so also here he reacted sharply to Janson's narrative intent:

Janson is a popular educator at the expense of the artist in him, and consequently at the expense of the poet. His works are a kind of secular parsonical poetry, but they are not art—not born of his absolute powers. One can see this throughout the whole of his production, and I myself have heard him say as much on many occasions: that it is a question of presenting the characteristic simplicities of life by the simplest means. No, it is not a question of that at all. It is a question of presenting the phenomena of life with artistry in such a way that it strikes home. *That* is what it is a question of.

There is in this phrase—'presenting the phenomena of life with artistry in such a way that it strikes home'—the germ of a policy that eventually determined his whole narrative strategy.

By artistry he meant that the novelist must repudiate the flatness and inertia of perfunctory and merely conceptual language, and apply himself diligently to the exploitation of all the subtleties that words are capable of:

> The poet must always, in every instance, have the vibrant word . . . that by its trenchancy can so wound my soul that it whimpers. . . . One must know and recognize not merely the direct but the secret power of the word; one must be able to give one's writing unexpected effects. It must have a hectic, anguished vehemence, so that it rushes past like a gust of air, and it must have a latent, roistering tenderness so that it creeps and steals into one's mind; it must be able to ring out like a sea-shanty in a tremendous hour, in the time of the tempest, and it must be able to sigh like one who, in tearful mood, sobs in his inmost heart. There are overtones and undertones in words and there are lateral tones.

And by 'the phenomena of life' he meant (as his later essay shows) things particular rather than general. What was so utterly repugnant to him was the notion that universality and general significance could be achieved only by a narrative simplification of certain views of life that were themselves absurdly over-simplified; discussions in conventional terms of simple morality seemed to him to be utterly without meaning when set against the richness and complexity of individual lives. Personal identity and the individual response were the real crux of things; and it was his conviction that the novel ought to extend to these previously almost neglected areas, the general range of human consciousness. There must be a stop put to the miserable traffic in 'types', in characters whose intellectual or emotional life was expressible— as he put it—'in whole numbers', in parsons who were wholly and merely the embodiment of religious orthodoxy, or women whose only thoughts day and night were of matrimonial felicity or infelicity. It was part of Strindberg's genius, Hamsun later declared, to have recognized and given expression to the psychological complexities, the broken and fragmented nature, of modern man: 'Strindberg is in my opinion about the only writer in Scandinavia who has made a serious attempt to produce modern psychology . . . Strindberg realizes—realizes and recognizes—the inadequacies of the character psychology prevailing at present for describing the split and disharmonic mind of modern man.' It was on this note that Hamsun concluded his case against Janson, in terms that carry an exhortation to the novelist to tell of the unique and the particular rather than of the conventional and the formulated, to deal rather with the concreteness of individual states of mind than with commonplace generalizations on 'typed' characters with their humdrum social life and betrothals and accidental misfortunes. And when he wrote there of the 'fractional feelings', when he claimed that there was that other 'unconscious and even today almost wholly uninterpreted life of the mind', he was using phrases that directly anticipate the arguments of his next important essay of two years later.

Perhaps the really significant thing about this next essay, 'From the Unconscious Life of the Mind', is not the light it sheds on Hamsun's own early work, revealing though that is, so much as its date: 1890. For here, as indeed in the early novels themselves, it is as though some of the catch-phrases current in Europe some twenty-five or thirty years later—those that tell of tracing the atoms as they fall upon the mind, of the disconnected and incoherent patterns scored on the unconscious, of the reveries between brackets of reality, of the tangles of mental association—were being given early rehearsal by him. He writes of the strange and inexplicable moods and thoughts that invade the mind, things that are often too elusive to be seized and held fast: 'They last a second, a minute, they come and go like a moving, winking light; but they have impressed their mark, deposited some kind of sensation, before they vanished.' If literature began to concern itself rather more with these states of mind, it would find itself treating individual events instead of barren generalizations and typifications, and would, he felt, acquire a greater relevance to what was important in modern life:

We would get to know a little about the secret stirrings that go on unnoticed in the remote parts of the mind, the incalculable chaos of impressions, the delicate life of the imagination seen under the magnifying glass; the random wanderings of those thoughts and feelings;

untrodden, trackless journeyings by brain and heart, strange workings of the nerves, the whisper of the blood, the entreaty of the bone, all the unconscious life of the mind.

It should not be overlooked that the assumptions which this essay makes about the sources of human thought and conduct had yet to be given the respectability of scientific support: the notion that much of human behaviour is the consequence of emotional phenomena; or that large areas of emotional life, because they are situated below the mind's conscious level, are not easily accessible to introspection; or that those phenomena residing in the subconscious or unconscious mind are not in themselves the marks of abnormality but are present in all men to a greater or lesser degree. What Hamsun is in fact asserting here is that an awareness of the true nature of this hidden part of life, and of the behaviour that has its roots therein, will assist the novelist towards a heightened form of 'reality', which in its rejection of commonplace incident will actually bring the novel closer to actual living and to the mode of existence of modern man.

'If you haven't, for fiction, the root of the matter in you,' wrote Henry James in the preface to *The Princess Casamassima*, 'haven't the sense of life and the penetrating imagination, you are a fool in the very presence of the revealed and assured; but if you are so armed, you are not really helpless, even before mysteries abysmal.' Faced with the abysmal mysteries of *Mysteries* (*Mysterier*, 1892), or even the disturbing strangeness of *Hunger* (*Sult*, 1890) and *Pan* (1894) and *Victoria* (1898), criticism has rarely shown impressive assurance. Whilst it would be impertinent as well as untrue to dismiss all criticism of the early Hamsun as unimaginative or helpless, nevertheless there may be detected even today remnants of a critical attitude to these works that is surely misconceived.

Henry James himself is in fact unexpectedly relevant to a discussion of these things; and between, for instance, *The Princess Casamassima* (1886) and Hamsun's novels of the 1890s, between the kinds of criticism they at times attracted, between the sorts of interpretation they properly deserved, and between the narrative

strategies that determined their mode of composition there are
similarities so striking as well as differences so fundamental
that a comparison of them is a source of much profit. Both James
and Hamsun drew the same reproach: that they were in their
work too contrived, too fantastic even, to be 'true'. Finding in
The Princess Casamassima a far from plausible story of conspiracy
and assassination, of secret aristocratic paternity, of what—even
as late as 1916—seemed to be grossly improbable social change,
even reputable criticism (as Lionel Trilling has pointed out)
found it 'wild' and 'distraught', discovered traces of 'perversities'
and characterized it as a 'bad dream'. Faced with a hero who
shoots himself in the foot merely because his rival in love is also
lame, or who carries a poison bottle in his waistcoat pocket ready
for use at all times, or who gives his last coppers to a stranger
whilst himself starving to death, who invents and enacts the most
intricate and meaningless schemes of bluff and deceit, Hamsun's
critics claimed to find there a strange species of pathological
creature, some perversely mysterious invention which, by all
common-sense standards, is beyond normal comprehension.

It is to this 'typical Hamsunesque hero' that attention has in
the main been addressed, and the chief aim of criticism the
compilation of a morbid case history. In one place, judgement is
passed by the standards of the social sciences, the conduct of the
hero in *Hunger* being described as 'such as to make the trained
social worker throw up his hands in holy horror and disgust'; in
another, authority is borrowed from medical science in order to
explain that the hero behaves as he does 'because the brain gets
too little blood when the body does not receive sufficient nourish-
ment'; the unspoken assumption all along being that to find a
common-sense and worldly excuse for these characters' behaviour is to 'explain' them, and when there is no obvious excuse
there is no explanation, only bewilderment. Nagel's conduct in
Mysteries is, according to one Norwegian critic, preposterous
because 'he has not—like the young man in Hamsun's first book
—any hunger to blame for all his absurdities; he is like that by
nature . . .'. And, almost as an abdication of criticism, we read a
point of view expressed in England: 'Tossed between all sorts of

contradictions, he [Nagel] can strike one as a genius manqué, a monomaniac, a romantic misanthrope, a posing charlatan, a lunatic—until the reader seems to lose all reliable clue to him. . . .'

It is almost beside the point to claim that just as events in Russia might be said to have 'justified' James's high-pressure plot, so Freud and the whole science of psycho-analysis has legitimized Hamsun's 'absurd' heroes. The view that sees little in *Hunger* but the story of a man of 'queer mental vagaries', or explains away Glahn in *Pan* as a man of 'strange erratic behaviour', or Nagel as somebody with a 'hopelessly unbalanced mind' is objectionable not because its conclusions, basing themselves as they do on the standards of ordinary, everyday practicality, are wholly untrue, but because any interpretation of these novels from naturalistic premises must necessarily overlook their true significance.

A valid reading requires us to look not so much at the hero as with him, in much the same way as a reading of *The Princess Casamassima* requires us to look not at the plot but through it. 'The value I wished most to render and the effect I wished most to produce', wrote Henry James of his novel, 'were precisely those of our not knowing, of society's not knowing, but only guessing and suspecting and trying to ignore what "goes on", irreconcilably, subversively, beneath the vast smug surface.' The difference between James and Hamsun is then seen to be one of territory and not of purpose; for instead of concerning himself with what goes on—and our attitudes to what goes on—behind the façade of society, Hamsun explores and shocks the reader into recognizing what goes on behind the mask of the individual. We look with the hero equally when he examines the secret areas within himself and when he looks at the world about him, a world in which the things of greatest significance are precisely those other secret mental lives of his fellows. It is this arrangement above all else that has given the richness to Hamsun's early work; and to realize this is to shift the search for the cause of its strange and arresting quality away from questions of character analysis and on to the more technical problems of narrative perspective. What we find in these novels is the secret history of a

number of unsuccessful personal campaigns; they feature the
intelligence work, the collection and collation of secret information, and the suppositions made from it; theirs is a record of
espionage and counter-espionage. What if the campaigns themselves end in defeat and disaster: in flight, as in *Hunger*; in
suicide, as in *Mysteries*; in despair and death, as in *Pan*; in a
broken heart, as in *Victoria*? What though the agent strikes some
as being a bit odd? The real business of these novels is not with
character-drawing nor with the chronicling of events, but with
secrets; and the intelligence work is at a level of sustained
brilliance.

The secrets are those that reside deep in personality, things
which human reticence normally keeps hidden or tries to ignore,
things repressed or camouflaged by social convention. By the
exercise of careful introspection, the central characters gain insight into the nature of these things, and submit to their compulsion; this is what one might call the primary stage of the
hero's encounter with life, a stage that finds its clearest expression
in *Hunger*. In the secondary and tertiary stages, the position is
more complex: from the knowledge the hero derives from his
introspective studies, from his understanding of the deeper
motives that influence human conduct, he is able—by close
observation, interrogation, and other methods familiar to the
secret observer—to acquire a sympathetic understanding of other
minds.

He places great reliance on trifles, those seemingly insignificant
events that reveal to the initiated the true nature of things more
surely than any of the more obvious outward signs. 'Don't neglect
trifles, my friend!' says Nagel to Minutten, 'for God's sake,
trifles have an enormous value.' Trifles, especially in Nagel's case
those subtler rhythms of human speech in which there is so often
an involuntary expression of something that overt behaviour is
perhaps at pains to conceal, are the medium of the self's betrayal.
Glahn uses different but comparable methods; an inclination of
the head, a flush of the cheek, a glance of the eye—these are the
signs to be marked and interpreted, this the material to speculate
on, this the code to which it often seems to him he possesses the

key. But in one respect he is even more explicit than Nagel: 'I believe that I can read a little of the mind of those people that I have to do with. . . . We sit in a room, a few men, a few women and I: and I seem to see what goes on within these people and what they think about me. . . . There I sit and watch all this and nobody suspects that I see through every mind. . . .' It is not only that Glahn is conscious of the secret power it gives him— or gives the illusion of giving him—over other people, making them transparent; but by concerning himself particularly with what they think about him, Glahn hints at his own vulnerability, his awareness that others might see through him unless he takes deliberate steps to prevent it. The natural reaction is seen most clearly in the case of Nagel; his defence is to contrive complicated plans of bluff and double bluff, to screen his own secret mental life by deliberate mystification whenever he has reason to believe himself observed; others shall see his foolings but not his feelings. To reveal one's inner soul to others without full control over the manner and the occasion of its revealing is, for him, to invite defeat in the game of love and life; some of the unconventional behaviour, much of the lying and deceit, most of the posing are thus deliberate distractions, a series of feint moves to baffle the hostile observer.

The point from which all else originates is what the hero 'thinks', using the term to include not merely processes of ratiocination but all the other phenomena of mental and emotional activity going on upon and below the surface of the mind. The novels offer the sum of an infinite series: what the hero thinks, what he thinks others think, what he thinks others think he thinks, and so on. When projected into action, this intense mental activity results in a two-ply pattern of conduct: from the precise observation and scrupulous recording of his own inner private life and dreams, there derives—if the term be allowed— their 'behaviouristic correlative', moments when the hero acts what he 'really' is without the supervention of any code of public conduct; and from his divining and evaluating of others' thoughts (and particularly of those thoughts directed towards his own person), there result those of his actions purposely intended to deceive in order that his own secret and private essence may be protected.

The reason why such a character is at first sight baffling is not that both forms of behaviour are remote from the conventional—which would merely justify our finding him 'eccentric'—but because they seem on the face of things to contradict each other. We are allowed a double perspective, but the picture we get of him in his private world seems to contradict the one we get of him in public; his conduct includes actions that appear inconsistent and even fantastic. But a good deal of it is controlled fantasy, an 'antic disposition' which makes his actions, if not predictable nor even explicable on common-sense grounds, then at least consistent with the fictional world that Hamsun has created. There is a kind of double exposure which, if viewed thus, resolves itself into a single and as it were stereoscopic image.

Inasmuch as he is poor, proud, intelligent, sensitive and to some extent set apart from his fellows, the hero of *Hunger* belongs to an established tradition in the novel; he shows a strong family resemblance to what Lionel Trilling, in writing of the nineteenth-century novel, has called the Young Man from the Provinces, a characteristic figure that he finds in Stendhal's *The Red and the Black*, Balzac's *Père Goriot* and *Lost Illusions*, Dickens' *Great Expectations*, Flaubert's *Sentimental Education*, and—with certain reservations—Tolstoi's *War and Peace* and Dostoevski's *The Idiot*. The provinciality of the hero, the thing that marks him off from the others, although possibly putting him at an initial disadvantage, yet equips him in some special way for the observing of society, need not—as Trilling himself has indicated—mean literally a provincial birth; in many instances it has happened that his 'province' has been social class. As an index of Hamsun's break with the tradition of a socially orientated literature, the 'provinciality' of his hero is neither that of geography nor that of class but of sensibility; it is not society that sets him apart but God: 'God had poked his finger into the network of my nerves and gently, casually even, had deranged the fibres a little. And God had withdrawn his finger; and look, there were some strands and fine roots on the finger from the fibre of my nerves. And there was an open hole left by the finger, which was God's finger; and a wound in the brain in the track of the finger' (Section 1). We have in a word, a shift of emphasis from the socially differentiated person who through experience is to learn the ways of society, to a psychologically differentiated person who through experience is to learn the mysterious ways of the mind.

Although there are many who will agree with Gabriel Scott in considering *Hunger* as 'Hamsun's most characteristic work', nevertheless the hero is still only at the apprentice stage of a training that is not fully developed until *Mysteries*; he is learning the secret melodies of the mind as they are played on his own jangled nerves. Hamsun, in a letter in which he wrote of *Hunger*, claimed that 'the book deliberately plays on a single string, but with an attempt to draw from that string hundreds of notes'. The physical torment of hunger, however large it may seem to bulk, plays only an incidental role; the actual theme of the novel, as Heiberg has rightly claimed, is that of privation at a number of levels—physical, erotic, social—and of an individual's struggle to build up an inner psychological defence against it. The mere fact of hunger is in itself something that a few kroner, borrowed or earned, can halt; its significance is as an agent of mental activity, bruising the mind in such a way as to make the hero excruciatingly sensitive to the touch of even the slightest things.

It is precisely by virtue of this painful sensitiveness that the hero 'lives'; he has no fictive life when his belly is filled or his pockets lined. Each of the four sections of the novel deals with a separate crisis of hunger; in the first three he is saved by getting his hands on a little money: payment for an article in the first, help from a friend in the second, charity from his editor in the third. When on the fourth occasion he rejects monetary help, the novel is at an end—he signs on as a deck-hand and sails out of the novel. Between whiles, in those weeks when he eats, there is no novel; the hero has ceased to be fictionally significant, has ceased to 'exist'.

His life is of the sort measured not by the clock or the calendar but by the intensity and refinement of his feelings and perceptions;

and as in the case of Nagel and Glahn, 'trifles' assume enormous significance. Minute impressions crowd in on him and he delights in the clarity with which he is able to record them: a dog brushing past, a yellow rose in a man's buttonhole set his thoughts vibrating and occupy him for long stretches of time. But in his case it is not merely that these trifles seize the imagination but that they also hurt:

There were natures that fed on trifles [the hero explains] and died for the sake of one hard word. And I implied that I had such a nature. The fact was that my poverty had so sharpened certain faculties in me that it caused me real discomfort: . . . But it also had its advantages, it helped me in certain situations. The intelligent poor man was a much more precise observer than the intelligent rich one. The poor man looks about him at each step he takes, listens suspiciously to every word he hears from every person he meets; every step he himself takes sets a problem for his thoughts and feelings, a labour. He is quick of hearing and sensitive, he is a man of experience, his soul bears the sear of the fire [Section 3].

His mind, to put it paradoxically, craves hunger, feeds on lack of food; starvation, however much it may weaken his bodily frame, alerts his mind, nourishes his powers of observation and heightens his consciousness.

His is a kind of involuntary decadence; had he elected to lead the life he does, his career might not have been so very dissimilar from that of many other fictional heroes of the 1890s. His mode of life bears a number of superficial resemblances to that of the orthodox decadents: a certain lack of proportion, a certain over-refinement of the sensibility, a recurring joy and astonishment at his own mental processes. But whereas the decadent, when the 'unwashed mood' was upon him, went slumming of his own volition, Hamsun's hero is cast down by a single rejection slip. There was no call for the hero of *Hunger* to seek vivid sensation, to court experience; where others had deliberate recourse to drugs and narcotics to extend their range of sensation and stimulate their reactions, hunger is enough for him; he sees no romance in the meanness and squalor of the capital, he is simply entrapped by it.

Hunger is then the account of a self-contained and self-conscious mind, a novel without a plot, without any orthodox development or culmination in the action, without moral lesson or social significance; it is not so much a shape or a construction as an extrusion chopped to a length. The hero enters into no dramatic relationship with any other character, but blunders into them and withdraws wounded; it is the record of a mind's impressions, a graph of unreason when set against the co-ordinates of polite social behaviour yet giving a clear and elegant demonstration of the problematic life of the individual, ambivalent soul. The world the hero inhabits is egocentric; the realism of 'things' in it is far removed from that sort of realism that addressed itself to the summarizing of outward detail of shape and colour, the sort Hamsun's contemporaries were accustomed to and which, according to Proust, is the sort 'furthest from reality'. It is a highly personal vision, the creation of a mind working on an empty stomach: cheap lodgings and police cells and a bench in the park, an arena where he can observe the play of his feelings and passion.

The novel is told as a first person narrative, a form which has often been held to lack authority or conviction because it offers the author no real detachment. In the case of *Hunger*, there is detachment of a kind in that there is a consistent division of self into two: one part of the hero's mind reacts instinctively and unthinkingly; and the other part is able to follow these reactions at a moment's interval of time, not close enough or decisively enough always to control or restrain them, but eagerly enough to be able to record them, and sufficiently aware of these processes to be able to reflect on them. 'I was [the hero confesses] fully conscious of playing a stupid joke without being able to do anything about it; my confusion ran away with me. . . . No matter how much I told myself I was behaving quite idiotically, it didn't help. . . . Involuntarily I lowered my head in shame.'

Avoidance of shame, the maintenance of his own peculiar standards of self-respect, is at the root of many of his actions in the first three-quarters of the book. Just as he is conscious of his own powers of observation, so also is he acutely and guiltily aware of being himself observed. Like the animals in a menagerie whom he pities because 'they know that people are standing look-ing at them' and because 'they feel the hundreds of curious glances and are affected by that', he constantly feels the eyes of others on him; and in his self-consciousness he begins to play a part, inventing books he is supposed to have written, profes-sions he is supposed to belong to, influential friends he is sup-posed to possess, false identities. It is in the changing attitude of his reflective self to this sort of conduct that any development the novel has must be sought; the hero changes in the course of the book not in the sense that his instincts and impulses vary but in respect of the attitudes adopted by the reflective self to the goings-on of its other half. It is a process of self-liberation, in which the freedom is that Hegelian freedom of the mind that comes with a knowledge of what the mind is up to and what its purposes are; and the working out of that process in the novel gives a classic instance of that state of affairs which Freud was later to analyse scientifically: the growth of feelings of guilt and shame as the tension between conscience and instinct is increased until, as the hero's understanding of the ways of the mind grows, there is movement across the frontier of conduct we have called shame, and self-censure gives place to self-marvel. What at first is 'weakness' or even 'madness' to him—that his thoughts should run so wildly at random and that his conduct should be so un-disciplined—is gradually incorporated into a private truth, into something which can even be exploited for gain, into a private protest against the levelling hand of society in the matter of morals.

It is true, as a perceptive Swedish critic has pointed out, that the salient thing about this character is his strength of will; and with this recognition comes the realization that the material distress he suffers is due not so much to the sheer pressure of circumstance as to his refusal to escape from distress by ways he considers unworthy or improper. But to go further and claim that in the end his moral resistance is broken is to misinterpret the whole direction of the novel. At the end of the book, it is true, we discover the hero permitting himself conduct that he would earlier, by the strength of his will and the compulsion of his moral sense, have forbidden himself; but this new attitude is the result not of any diminution of his will power or any falling off in his standards but to a change—a refinement he might well claim—in his moral outlook. He no longer shares the standards of the masses; he has, through experience, won the knowledge of his own uniqueness and with it come into possession of a unique moral code. The aristocratic pride that initially marked him off from other men by sustaining him where others, in similar extreme conditions, would have succumbed is later intensified; and by acting as previously he would not have acted, he distinguishes himself yet again and on an even higher plane from what he himself was earlier and from those few others like him.

He emerges from his experiences with a completely new view of public standards of conduct, with little sense of conventional shame, and with a willingness to accept as beneficial the previously incomprehensible workings of his mind. But in what way beneficial? It is not until *Mysteries* that the thing is plainly stated: 'Do you know what a great poet is?' asks Nagel. 'Well, a great poet is a person who has no shame, who never blushes.' To the more obvious up and down movement of the novel, the rise and fall in intensity in step with the successive stages of hunger and repletion there is therefore added this forward movement of initiation: an initiation not, as had been traditional, into the ways of society and public truth but into the ways of the individual mind and of private truth.

Mysteries was planned as something psychological in temper and exclusive in appeal.

It is to be a psychological novel [Hamsun wrote to Marie Herzfeld on 10 August 1890]. Actually I am working very slowly; I am completely incapable of writing for the masses; novels with betrothals and dances and childbirth, overlaid with an external apparatus, are a bit too cheap for me and have no interest for me. With the little I do accomplish, I address myself to an intellectual *élite*, and it is the appreciation of this *élite* that I value. But it is for this reason I write so slowly.

At the very outset, the fictional narrator of *Mysteries* puts his own construction on the 'facts' of Nagel's career. Listen, he says,

to the strange events that took place last summer in a little
Norwegian coastal town: 'There popped up in the town a
stranger, a certain Nagel, a remarkable and peculiar charlatan,
who did a lot of extraordinary things and who disappeared again
just as suddenly as he had come.' The account of these 'facts' is
both privileged and on the whole fair, and we are by some dis-
pensation allowed direct access on at least two occasions to the
flow of Nagel's secret thoughts; the teller does not, outside the
first paragraph, permit himself to pass judgement on Nagel's
behaviour and is content to record faithfully the other characters'
opinions of and responses to this strange phenomenon. But because his mind at least is made up, because he has translated to
his own satisfaction what Nagel does and thinks into what he *is*,
his narrative is unconsciously biased; because Nagel is prejudged,
the account fails to attach importance to certain things that might
otherwise have been thought significant; the consequence is that
the reader is challenged to review the 'facts' and to construct for
himself the reality behind them.

'I am thinking about what was said about Nagel this after-
noon', says Dagny to Martha on the final page of the novel, some
months after Nagel has thrown himself into the harbour to his
death. 'But one thing they did not know. Nagel told me as early
as last summer that Minutten would come to a bad end. I do
not know how he could see all that. He said it long before you
told me what Minutten had done to you.' In spite of the general
view of Nagel held by the community—that he was an unbalanced eccentric or worse—Dagny knows that in one significant respect Nagel was right, and could now be proved right
where everybody else was wrong; he alone had been convinced
of Minutten's evil disposition, the meek and humble Minutten,
who at all times was solicitous of the well-being of others, who
never withheld his forgiveness from those who had ill-treated
him, who had the sympathy of all right-thinking people. How
Nagel knew, and the merits of his way of knowing, and the consequence of his knowing in this way, these are the questions that
lead straight to the heart of the novel and bring to the surface
those things that Hamsun was concerned to say in it.

Nagel's knowledge of Minutten's secret ways was not gained by any of the (to others) reliable methods of logic or deduction or indeed any form of ratiocination; his conclusions were against all reason, against all the evidence, even that of his own dreams; he had kept this man under the closest observation, laid secret traps for him, interrogated him skilfully and at length, but still he had no vestige of proof for what he knew to be true; he would not himself have objected to the trite explanation that he knew 'in his heart', but would have strongly resisted any insinuation that his method of knowing was inferior to any of those that generally enjoy the reputation of greater reliability. It was simply that he was certain.

The proofs he lived by were in essence quite different from those that carried conviction with other men, from all those that in his view were either the waste products of habitual and short-visioned 'thinking' or else the equally inadequate and superficial findings of the scientific intellect. He is passionate in his denunciation of the uncritical acceptance by his fellow-men of truths that get handed down without any real scrutiny: 'What does the world know? Nothing! People just become used to things, they accept them, acknowledge them because their teachers have acknowledged them before, everything is supposition pure and simple, even time and space and motion and mass are supposition, the world knows nothing, it just accepts.' He gloats when raw superstition and quackery work where the Doctor's pills fail; he becomes exasperated with those who regard the multiplication table as the high road to wisdom; his renunciation of science is as passionate and instinctive as D. H. Lawrence's cry 'All scientists are liars'. His way of knowing is the prerogative of what Eduard von Hartmann had defined as the 'mystical' mind. Basing himself on Schelling, and claiming that the essence of the mystical is 'the filling of the consciousness with a content . . . through involuntary emergence of the same from the Unconscious', Hartmann denoted as mystical those thoughts and feelings which are independent of any laboriously logical and rational process, which are apprehended by immediate feeling and which owe their origin to an immediate intrusion of the Unconscious.

There are other reasons for suspecting that Nagel is to some extent constructed on Hartmann's ideas; and for suspecting that this—in part at least—is the way we are intended to see him. Nagel seems at times to reveal clairvoyant gifts; he enters a building and knows in some strange way that it has at some time been used as a chemist's shop; he passes a man on the street and something tells him this man is called Johannes even though this fact is not generally known in the community. Every man, says Hartmann, carries about with him a sense of the recurring mysteries of the unconscious, but only those who possess the power of clairvoyance and presentiment are worthy of the name of mystic; and he adds that one of the more characteristic manifestations of the mystic mind is its tendency towards pictorial-symbolic expression, a tendency that in Nagel with his stories and his predilection for symbol and metaphor is fully developed. Both in the manner of his expression and in his occasionally unusual powers of vision he betrays qualities that hint at the possession of 'mystical' gifts.

Hartmann is careful to distinguish these genuine marks of mysticism from what he calls its excrescences—convulsions, epilepsies, ecstasies, hysteria and so on—things which, although not central to mysticism, nevertheless often accompany it and do not necessarily invalidate its power. The relevance of this distinction to any analysis and interpretation of Nagel's behaviour is obvious. Partly to enhance the sense of mystery that attaches to him, partly to mark himself off from the common herd, and partly to win tactical advantages in the battle of life, he goes in for deliberate mystification; his exhibitionism is an excrescence, deliberately fostered, on his way of life and thought. It is, however, a mode of living that has its inevitable dangers, and his gifts, such as they are, urge him relentlessly on to extremes of unreason; so that, to use Hartmann's phrase, 'mysticism spontaneously degenerates into the morbid'. Nagel is not exempt from this process; it threatens him throughout his stay in the town and it is this that finally takes possession of him and draws him to his death.

The traffic in mystery in this novel is therefore two-way. There is the mystery that things unconventional or extraordinary have for the common sense or 'realistic' mind, like the mystery in Nagel's claim to have been sailing 'in a boat of scented wood with a sail of light blue silk cut in the shape of a crescent moon', which the honest sanity of his fellows can only greet with embarrassed perplexity or dismiss as an 'hallucination'; this is the mystery that Nagel is at pains to foster and exploit for his own advantage. And on the other hand, there is the mystery which the commonplace always holds for the exceptional or 'mystical' mind; the mystery that exists eternally for a mind which, as Nietzsche puts it, knows how 'every opinion is also a lurking place, every word is also a mask'. Each side therefore finds a strange fascination in the other: society living in a world of soluble problems, Nagel living among half-perceived mysteries; society putting its trust in science and the exercise of reason, Nagel putting faith in wisdom and the cultivation of intuition.

Nagel's seemingly perverse and irresponsible actions are, however, in the light of this, not the real mysteries but merely an accompaniment to them; the genuine mysteries are those which Hartmann claims are recurrent in every man: the apparently inexplicable grounds for human thoughts and desires and conduct, the 'reality' that scientific method is too coarse-meshed to catch, the 'subjective logic of the blood' as Nagel puts it, the intrusion into everyday actions of the secret workings of the unconscious. Nagel's career is an appeal for attention to something rather like what Wordsworth called 'unknown modes of being', for an alerted and sensitive awareness of the mysteries that lurk below the surface, behind the face, beyond the horizon, everywhere outside that little patch of life trampled bare by crude common sense. What did we really gain even in a purely practical sense, Nagel asks, by stripping life of all poetry, all dreams, all beautiful mysticism, all lies? 'What is truth?' he goes on, 'Can you tell me that? We advance only by means of symbols, and we change these symbols as we progress.' These are the mysteries that Nagel both feels in himself and is aware of in others, the blind forces of life; these are the things his story-telling illustrates, his opinions reflect and his career enacts. He flays the smugness of those who live by commonplace truth, who in their *Seminaristvisdom* are so sure of themselves, for he knows that the deeper verities can only be expressed in dreams and symbols and lies. But he lives this life of dream and superstition and impulse not because he is a genuinely naïve person but because he is super-sophisticated, he lives (and dies) by his trinkets and charms not because he is ignorant of the discipline of rational logic but because he consciously rejects it as a valid mode of existence. His illogical behaviour incorporates a kind of super-logic and derives from his acknowledgement of the ambivalence that invades all aspects of life that have to do with human conduct. He is deep in the tradition of those who champion the instinct against the mind; he is the prophet of irrationalism.

He is, however, a minor prophet; indeed he fails even to be that. And it is this fact that makes *Mysteries* a novel not a philosophical treatise, and lends richness to it. Nagel wears ideas that are too big for him; he casts himself in the mould of the exceptional man as Nietzsche defined him in *Die fröhliche Wissenschaft*, but the proportions are mean and the material base. He pops up —and both Hamsun (*dukket opp*) and Nietzsche (*auftauchen*) use nearly identical terms—in the little provincial town with his atavistic ideas in a way that is almost a parody of Nietzsche's words:

Die seltenen Menschen einer Zeit verstehe ich am liebsten als plötzlich auftauchende Nachschösslinge vergangener Kulturen und deren Kräften: gleichsam als den Atavismus eines Volkes und seiner Gesittung . . . . Jetzt erscheinen sie fremd, selten, ausserordentlich: und wer diese Kräfte in sich fühlt, hat sie gegen eine widerstrebende andere Welt zu pflegen, zu verteidigen, zu ehren, grosszuziehen: und so wird er damit entweder ein grosser Mensch oder ein verrückter und absonderlicher, sofern er überhaupt nicht beizeiten zugrunde geht . . .

Nagel is a small-time Zarathustra, a prophet of the provinces, a thinker (as he himself puts it) who has never learned to think, a man who, had his stature been greater, might have proclaimed new laws for humanity but who, with things as they are, is able to sustain his being 'different' only by fooling his fellow-men: 'He had had such absurdly beautiful dreams of achieving something on earth, something that would "count", some exploit that the meat-eaters could be scandalized at—and it had turned out badly; he had not been equal to the task.' The proud slogan of 'Umwertung aller Werte' degenerates into the more comfortable 'épater le bourgeois'. 'Man, thy name is donkey', Nagel tells himself. 'You can be led by the nose wherever one likes.'

Like Lawrence—who said: 'My neighbour to me is mean and detestable'—Nagel is critical of his fellow-men often to the point of hatred, yet responds with humility to nature and all that is creative and organic. Like Nietzsche and like Dostoevski's Raskolnikow, he divides up the world into the masses on the one hand and a few outstandingly great men on the other; he talks big about the need for some great deed, some colossal crime even that would reveal true greatness; but he himself shrinks from the deed that would achieve this and he has throw-backs to dreams of an idyllic life in the forest. His is no Dostoevskian 'will to self-assertion', nor any Nietzschean 'will to power'; it is simply the will to be different.

The bizarre and futile scheming and the barely concealed arrogance of this character together form the response, to some of the most devastating ideas of the age, of a mind wholly unequal to them. He is an exhibitionist who tries to exploit his exhibitionism in order to control the course of his life and the lives of those about him. He wants both to know what they think (and therefore how they will behave) and also to control their thinking. He becomes obsessed with trivialities—'the human soul', he says, '. . . no trifle is without relevance to it, everything has some significance for it'—fearful lest any small thing that might truly reveal should ever escape him, and building enormous edifices of conjecture on trifling evidence. He engineers a reputation for himself on the basis first of creating and then of dashing and then again fulfilling certain anticipations in respect of his own person. On his arrival he impressed the locals by having among his luggage a violin case, then allows it to be known that all it contains is dirty washing, so that when he seizes a violin at the local bazaar and runs through a piece or two with some competence he is hailed as a virtuoso. After he has nobly and courageously intervened to save Minutten from the attentions of a drunken tormentor, he reports on the incident to Dagny in terms that show his own role in a bad light, knowing full well that she has already been given some other account of the incident. 'Why do you lie about yourself?' asks Dagny. He explains that he tells such lies in a spirit of speculation, trying to get all possible profit for himself out of the affair. And when Dagny further asks why, if that was indeed his idea, did he go and spoil it all by revealing his methods, his answer is that that too was calculated. Everything, his unconventional clothes, his astonishing behaviour, his indiscretions, all are calculated, even the confession of his calculating methods.

But with what object? It is an aspect of his unrelenting struggle to impose a strict control on his own world. He attempts to grapple with life's problems, not like the heavy-weight wrestler but like the Judo expert, luring the world about him off its two-footed stability so that a slight push and he has it where he wants it. But by his very insight into the ways of the soul, he must know the impossibility of his task; his awareness of the disruptive power of the unconscious, both on his own emotions and on those of others, shows him to be trying to govern the ungovernable, predict the unpredictable.

The antagonistic tension that exists between Nagel and Minutten is one of Hamsun's chief devices for giving sharpness and definition to the philosophy of life that Nagel stands for, or one should rather say ultimately lacks the inner strength to stand for. Nagel, who seeks to command life, who is ruthless and cunning in his small way when he tries to impose his will on others, who is arrogant and wholly impatient of those who do not share his views, but who is nevertheless soft-hearted and generous in secret and desperately anxious that he should not be discovered as such, is a deficient Nietzschean. Minutten, who shows all the virtues of meekness and humility and selflessness, who is submissive and makes what he can of those things life allows him, but who is nevertheless capable of secret evil, is an imperfect Christian. Nagel sees in him an opponent of equal resourcefulness; Minutten has 'fooled' him—in the matter of the poison bottle—as successfully as ever Nagel 'fooled' the others, a thing which, much as it has exasperated him, he cannot help but admire. He despises Minutten and yet fears him at the same time; he was at one stage even moved to hint at a pact of non-aggression between them. Both have roles to play; both play them consistently, for just as Minutten cannot be lured into a single thoughtless move, so Nagel plays his part even when alone in his room and seemingly safe from observation; but whereas Nagel's is active deception, a succession of feint moves, Minutten's is a kind of passive camouflage; and although their tactics are different, they fight with the same weapons and they know it.

Nagel does in his own small way and in his limited surroundings what Hamsun saw Strindberg doing in his; and the terms Hamsun used of Strindberg are not inappropriate to Nagel: 'One would have to be a naïve person if one simply took all Strindberg's paradoxes at their face value; but on the other hand one would have to be a stupid person if one did not at the same time realize that one was here faced with an energetic and extremely acute observer who, by thrusting his way in everywhere and blowing off the dust, has sniffed out an abundance of observations about a number of things.' Nagel is also a 'fractional' character, not to be added up in whole numbers, but 'inconsistent' only if one attempts to measure him by some conventional and common-sense moral scheme—an undertaking that would be entirely contrary to Hamsun's own view of the exploratory nature of psychological literature. And again it is something from Lawrence, his idea of the allotropy of the ego, the variation of external properties and characteristics without any real change of substance, that aids understanding: 'You mustn't look in my novel for the old stable ego of the character', wrote Lawrence; 'There is another *ego*, according to whose action the individual is unrecognizable, and passes through, as it were, allotropic states which it needs a deeper sense than we have been used to exercise, to discover are states of the same single radically unchanged element.' Thus, to adapt Lawrence's terms, the exercise of a deeper critical sense brings the realization that Nagel is neither diamond nor soot, neither a brilliant thing of many facets nor a shapeless smudge, but carbon—carbon which as diamond and soot and graphite and charcoal is always the same thing but different. Nagel's career is capable of being interpreted with equal validity as the reaction of a broad and generous mind to the stuffy and restricting ways of a small and ingrowing community, and as the nervous, hectic projection of a lonely, unintegrated, divided mind. And it was surely the author's intention that it should be so.

The temptation to read too much into the title of *Pan* is great and not without danger. That there is deliberate exploitation of symbolism in the novel as a whole, there can be no doubt; and Hamsun, who claimed to have fashioned this novel with the same care as he would a poem, striving all the time to give the language of it some of the suggestive power of poetry, would not himself have objected to a critical approach that put great reliance on the interpretation of its symbols; in a letter to Albert Langen, later his German publisher, on 2 September 1894, he wrote about these things: 'The reason why my book is not yet complete is that each chapter is a poem, each line of which has been carefully gone over. There are no conversations in it, only an occasional exchange of words. When I tell you that each chapter has cost me a week's work, I do not lie, even though the chapters are so short. The thing progresses but, I must say, slowly.' But as a check on attaching too great significance to the title one must remember that it was probably not chosen until the novel was complete. In the same letter, Hamsun mentions his uncertainty about what the title should be; he had considered calling the book 'Edvarda' but hesitated because he felt she was not altogether central to the book. The evidence of this letter invites one to see the title as something subsequently chosen as appropriate to the complete novel rather than to approach the novel as a premeditated treatment of the spirit of Pan in the modern world. Although Pan may be rightly seen as belonging to the same kin as Dionysus and Orpheus in that he, like them, stands for a distinctive attitude to the world, an attitude that in the most general of terms may be said to be hostile to rationalism, he does not occupy the same central place in the thought of Hamsun as

Dionysus and Orpheus do in the thought of Nietzsche and Rilke.

There is, of course, one level of interpretation to which Pan quite obviously and properly belongs: the spirit of Pan fills the Nordland forest where Glahn elects to live. Glahn who possesses a powder-horn with the figure of Pan on it, finds himself wondering as he sits in the forest thinking his thoughts: 'Was Pan sitting in a tree watching to see how I would act? And was his belly open; and was he crouching so that he seemed to sit and drink from his own belly? But all this he did just to keep one eye cocked on me; and the whole tree shook with his silent laughter when he saw all my thoughts running away with me.' Glahn leads a life wholly in the spirit of Pan, calls himself 'a son of the forest', he hunts and shoots and fishes, and he disports himself with the forest maidens. But the deeper implications of *Pan* are not so much Pantheistic as pantheistic; and one must acknowledge not merely the horned and bearded Pan but also the 'pan' of the ἐυ καὶ πάν, the Universal and All-embracing. In another letter to Albert Langen, on 22 July 1894, Hamsun wrote: 'I write, things progress slowly but well. I find it difficult to give it a title. I think of the Northern parts of Norway, the regions of the Lapps, the secrets and wide-spread superstition, the midnight sun; I think of J. J. Rousseau in these parts making the acquaintance of a Nordland girl—that is my book. I am trying to present something of the nature worship, the sensibility, the supersensitiveness of a Rousseau-like soul.' Glahn is then a child of Nature, ill at ease in society, a modern Werther with a dog for companionship instead of an Ossian, a soul that seeks its fulfilment in the forest and in solitude, a mind that at moments of heightened sensibility is capable of a kind of mystical union with nature and the universe: 'Listen in the east,' he cries, sitting alone at night in the forest, 'and listen in the west, but listen! That is the everlasting God. This stillness in my ear is the blood of all nature seething, is God weaving through the world and through me.' His senses throb in rhythm with the great stillness of the forest; a strange rush of air calls to him and he feels himself transported, pressed to an invisible breast—God was stand-

ing near. God is the immanent principle in Glahn's universe, is
in the world and of it, is 'the wind and the stars, . . . the dust of
the road and the leaves that fall, . . . the twelve months and the
ships at sea', is the mysterious God of life and the heart. The
novel contrives a single unity of nature and human nature; it is
permeated with the slow rhythm of the birth and death of the
Nordland landscape, with the rise and fall of passion.

The connection between the pantheism of *Pan* and the doctrine of the unconscious which Hamsun had selected as the
proper basis of literature may not be immediately obvious. But
it is real, and the link between them is one that Eduard von
Hartmann had already forged. Claiming at the time of his writing
that 'the more special forms of the Christian religion are mani-
festly outlived', Hartmann wrote:

We stand directly before the time when the Jewish–Christian cosmic
theory has only the choice of *dying out entirely or becoming pantheistic.*
The metaphysical foundation of the transformation, however, which
was prepared by the pantheistic and mystical philosophies of the Middle
Ages and the Reformation . . . has been philosophically laid and built
on by the most recent German philosophers, whose partially justified
and valuable endeavours and tendencies have coalesced into a provisional
unity in the principle of the Unconscious.

If then we accept as true the notion that all Hamsun's early
novels deal with various aspects of the unconscious, then we
may say that in *Hunger* we read its morality, in *Mysteries* its
psychology, and in *Pan* its metaphysic.

Glahn cannot, however, by any stretch of imagination be
thought of as a primitive, as a noble savage. He is different and
knows he is different from the simple, almost plant-like people
he comes to live among in the land of the midnight sun: 'The
people I met were strange; they seemed to have a different nature
from any I had known before. Sometimes a single night was
enough to make them blossom out from childhood in all their
glory, mature and fully grown.' The rhythm of their lives was
different, the whole pattern of behaviour dominated by the
passage of the sun. After the brief and hectic summer and with

the coming of the first snow Glahn noticed that 'a mysterious stillness came over the people, they brooded in silence, their eyes waited for the winter. . . . Everything was making ready for the endless night of the Northern lights when the sun slept in the sea.' Henriette, the goatherd girl who gave herself readily to him in the summer, now ignores his invitation in silence: 'The autumn, the winter has laid hold of her, already her senses were aslumber. Already the sun had gone into the sea'. It brings an echo of the mocking differentia of Beaumarchais: 'Boir sans soif, et faire l'amour en tout temps, c'est ce qui distingue l'homme de la bête'; even in this Henriette is closer to the primitive, the animal existence than is Glahn.

It is only in a very limited sense that one can describe Glahn as a child of nature; certainly he is not (as one critic has asserted) 'a backward child' nor is he a simple child; he is a highly complex, introspective reversion to childhood; his fate is not the loss of inborn innocence but the precipitate of his own dæmonic, even pandæmonic nature. 'Sie werden entweder Natur sein', said Schiller in defining what he called 'naïve' types, 'oder sie werden die verlorene suchen', meaning those whom he designated as 'sentimentalisch'. Glahn is not 'naïve' as Eva and Henriette are, is not 'the ecstatic child of Life', but he obeys his 'sentimentalisch' urge to seek Nature, renouncing the world of culture and attempting to find reconciliation with the great solitude. The idyllic picture Nagel had drawn to Martha Gude of life with her in the forest here finds a partial realization, Nagel's vision is in large measure Glahn's reality; and the equilibrium Glahn finds in the forest might have remained if he had been left to share it with a Martha or an Eva, or a Henriette; but for reasons that torment him and that are not really 'reasons' at all, he finds the attraction of the complex personality of Edvarda overwhelming; she is the catalyst, the introduction of which into the chemistry of Glahn's existence changes the slow fusion of his soul with the great oneness of nature into a violent reaction that ends only with his own disintegration.

The qualities of mind and temperament that Glahn possesses make their contribution to his fate. His acute sensitiveness, which is the source of his delight in nature but which torments him in his role of lover, is perhaps the chief of these; and it is significant to see the phrase that David Hume used of Rousseau—who he claimed had been born 'without a skin'—finding an echo in the words of Hans Brix: 'In his first person novels, Hamsun strips off from his own Self the official outer surface and thereby presents a figure whose nerves and blood-vessels lie exposed and quivering.' In his impulsiveness, Glahn is often driven to act in ways that society can neither understand nor easily forgive; as when he seizes Edvarda's shoe in a pique and flings it into the sea; or when, sickened by the humiliations he suffers at a party, he quietly walks over to the Baron as though to whisper something and spits in his ear. He also has all those qualities of personal magnetism that Goethe associated with 'das Dämonische', qualities that give their possessor such astonishing powers over others but which contain the seed of self-destruction; the circumstances of Glahn's death, which he himself contrives and is able to engineer precisely by virtue of his power over other men, exploiting his personal magnetism as the very instrument of his self-wrought death, are peculiarly 'dæmonic'. But to see the particular and individual traits peculiar to Glahn as the source of the catastrophic climax of the novel—as Landquist has argued with much persuasiveness—is to particularize too much the thing this novel is trying to communicate. For *Pan* is first and foremost a love story, a story of 'mind-perverted, will-perverted, ego-perverted love'.

An account of the love of Glahn and Edvarda in the vocabulary of Jungian psychology would probably claim that they each project their ideals on the other and are disappointed; that Glahn attaches with disastrous results his *anima*, his image of Woman, to Edvarda, and that she in return reacts unconsciously to the disparity between her *animus*, her image of Man, and the individual that is Glahn. It is the Doctor who sees most clearly the conflict in Edvarda's soul and the contradictions in her; he explains how she had formed an ideal and thought to find it realized in Glahn, the man with the 'animal look', and how it was this ideal that perverted her love. Glahn's *anima* receives no

10

direct analysis in the novel such as the Doctor gives of Edvarda; instead it is presented indirectly in the dreams and fantasies about Iselin as they take shape in Glahn's mind; Iselin, who comes to her new lover with a bold invitation in her eye and with ready surrender in her heart, who leaves her room unbarred, who bolts the door behind her lover as he enters 'as a small service to him', who is 'exulting and sinful from head to foot'. When this inner picture of Woman is unconsciously projected on to Edvarda, a slip of a girl, tall but with no figure, for whom he feels sympathy because she looked forlorn, whose thumb had a chaste and girlish look and who had kindly wrinkles on her knuckles, the result is disastrous.

Pan is the story of what happens to love when it ceases to be a simple coming together between man and woman, ceases to be even an animal desire for sexual satisfaction and becomes very largely a desire to be loved by someone else as a matter of personal pride; and when it is made, even unconsciously, the object of calculation or an ideal, when as D. H. Lawrence put it:

> . . . the mind interferes with love, or the will fixes on it,
> or the personality assumes it as an attribute, or the ego takes
>   possession of it,
> it's not love any more, it's just a mess.

With both Glahn and Edvarda, the disintegration of love begins with its declaration; once they begin to feel sure of the other person, their love is, as Lawrence says elsewhere in his poem, 'a cold egg'. And such is the complexity of their feelings that after the first passionate and reciprocal declaration of love, the whole affair develops into a desperate and inexorable drama of alternating doubt and reassurance, attraction and repulsion, love and hate; assurance kills this sort of love, and even though doubt can momentarily revivify it, it dies again with further reassurance. All in all, it is a view of love that strikes the present-day reader as having a strangely existentialist flavour, reminding him of Sartre's claim that 'love is self-frustration', something that thrives on frustration and discord and has as its object its own defeat.

Victoria, which bears the sub-title 'A love story', is a variation on the same theme: 'I hope to have my new book ready by the end of the month', Hamsun wrote to Albert Langen from Nord Aurdal on 27 September 1898, 'a novel, a kind of "pendant" to *Pan*, but less extensive'. Once again the lovers fail to find each other. It might seem on the surface that it is merely a social barrier that keeps Johannes, the miller's son, from marrying Victoria, the daughter of the big house, even after he has achieved some fame as a poet and author. In his imagination, in the 'novel within a novel' he is portrayed as writing, Johannes pictures Victoria as being in a walled garden; only the wall, the barrier of social inequality, he feels, keeps them apart. But although this is a factor of some significance, and although there is even greater compulsion on Victoria of a more sordid nature—from her father who needs a rich son-in-law to avert bankruptcy—nevertheless *she* sees more clearly than anyone what it is that really stands in the way of their happiness: 'Dear God, you must know how I have loved you, Johannes', she writes in a letter shortly before her death, 'I have never been able to show it, so much has stood in my way, most of all my own nature'. She, too, finds herself embroiled in a mind-perverted love; she, too, learns that love, the only kind of love she is capable of, is self-frustration.

The letter which Victoria writes and which concludes the novel is a new departure in Hamsun, slight but significant in its way. In none of the other novels we have been considering has the reader ever been allowed a glimpse of woman as she is in her own right, so to speak; neither Ylajali nor Dagny nor Edvarda nor any of the others have been permitted to express themselves independently, and (as Hanna Astrup Larsen pointed out) all their words and deeds have been recorded only after having been projected through the prism of the mind of some male character; all we see of Dagny is what Nagel sees of Dagny, of Edvarda what Glahn sees. The perspective throughout all these novels is that of the man, the worlds these novels severally create are male worlds, and their technical structure such as to remind one again of the concept of the *anima*. Obviously it does not in all cases necessarily follow that the fictional *anima* of the hero coincides with the actual *anima* of the author; but in this case it surely does. Dagny and Edvarda and to some extent also Victoria embody the views on women Hamsun was known to hold and to which he gave expression in his Strindberg article in 1894; there he claimed that woman is inferior to man, physically and intellectually, and that she is therefore driven to exercise a tyranny over him by unworthy methods: 'She is weaker than the man, therefore she must resort to baser methods: she caresses, coaxes, kisses, weeps, howls, screams, intrigues her way towards her goal —and the man bows and sidles along, because it is a woman.'

The reader seeks in vain for any objective or non-partisan picture of women and their modes of thinking and doing; the very structure of the first-person novels prevents it from being otherwise in them; and even where the third-person technique is adopted, the reader is allowed to know of the secret dreams and thoughts of the male hero (including his dreams and thoughts of women) in a way he is denied with the female characters. Until, on the last few pages of *Victoria*, the heroine is permitted a self-expression and a self-analysis which, even though it is only in the form of a letter, has no serious precedent in the novels here considered. Is it reading too much into this to see it as the first tentative step away from the narrowly focused sympathies and perspectives of the early works to the broader sweep of the later ones, works that derive from an imaginative insight into minds other than that of a super-sensitive, egocentric bachelor of about thirty?

To set these novels in a European perspective is to see the young men in them looking back to those of their kind who had gone before, at Pip and David Copperfield and Keller's Green Henry and all that generation constituting the spiritual heirs of Julien Sorel and Wilhelm Meister: and to see them anticipating by some twenty or thirty years the heroes of the later generation of which Swann and Josef K. and Stephen Dedalus are the greatest and most representative.

The fact is possibly worth pondering that *Hunger* stands almost exactly midway in time between *Great Expectations* and *Ulysses*, between a declaration that society owes its promise of genteel living to the existence of a shabby underworld of filth and squalor and a declaration that the individual, if he is to realize himself, must acknowledge a hidden and often murky substratum of the soul. For however much the classic novel of the nineteenth century, the *Bildungsroman* and its many modifications, might seem to tell a tale of a hero and his career, the silent centre of the work is generally society, into the established ways and values of which the hero is initiated; the social order is envisaged as something for him to discover or to reform or to accuse or to come to terms with, something that, whatever the personal attitudes adopted towards it, is yet conceived as an abiding thing, an axis about which personalities and events may turn. By the second and third decades of this present century, the roles in the novel of society and individual had been largely reversed, the custody of life's integrities had passed from society to individual, and the hero's value to the novel was assessed by the extent of his command over some unique perception of life and the things around him; he was seen as the embodiment of some secret essence that not merely determined his view of the world but even in a great measure itself created that world; things were no longer there just to be explored: the world was as the hero made it and each novel made it anew. It was to this fundamental change in the tradition of the novel that Hamsun contributed with his earliest writing, a contribution that was remarkable for the vigour with which its innovations were presented.

How far such a change is—to use the unfashionable but not wholly meaningless terms—a question of content or a question of style is no simple matter to decide. But in so far as one is able to isolate problems of narrative technique, there is one aspect of Hamsun's work that merits greater recognition than it is usually given: the historical importance of his contribution to the development of the 'stream of consciousness' technique. Precise definition of the term is, and no doubt will continue to be, a matter for dispute; but there is beginning to emerge some agreement about what properly belongs to the history of the thing it stands for. It is rare, however, and much rarer than is proper, that Hamsun's name joins the debate; for this technique is not only employed intermittently in all the four early novels considered here, but is also boldly exploited in two remarkable passages (chaps. 4 and 18) in *Mysteries*, i.e. in 1892, passages that reveal an audacity in the matter of free association that one normally attributes to works of a much later date; they offer a direct and only partially edited report of the musings of the mind, a random journey without maps, movement without purpose, nor is there at any time any intervention on the part of the author, there is no comment and no attempt at interpretation. In these inner monologues, the modernity of the idiom is unmistakable.

What follows from these recognitions? Perhaps first a warning: that it is invitingly easy to make, and not difficult to document, a number of persuasive and possibly extravagant claims on behalf of Hamsun: to suggest that his thought is Bergsonian before Bergson, Freudian before Freud; to discover in his technique an anticipation of Proust and Joyce and Virginia Woolf; to recognize, in the disinterested subjectivity of his brand of truth, the calculating irrationality of his characters and the reactionary radicalness of his authorship something of the ambivalence that is the keynote of the literature of the new century.

The graph of Hamsun's authorship, from the challenging experimentalism of *Hunger* and the novels of the 1890s to the subdued accomplishment of the August trilogy and the 1930s, has therefore its origin in a revolt against ageing fashion; and yet its terminus is found to lie in a disregard for the newly-won tradition that Hamsun himself helped to inaugurate. To claim this is to make a statement of a different order from, say, those that discover in his work a progression from the subjective to the objective, or from the analytical to the synoptic, or from an interest in individual and particular minds to a preoccupation with communal and generalized behaviour; for in selecting 'fashion' and 'tradition' as co-ordinates, one takes values that are—swiftly and erratically in one case, slowly and by accretion in the other—continually shifting and yet which are somehow reflected in each other. Nevertheless a chart of the novels of middle and later life shows a steady withdrawal from the extreme position he contested in his early work; inner motive is no longer stripped bare, there is a thick overlay of external incident, the depersonalization of style is taken so far that many of his early strictures of others might well be applied to his own later work. And that is the final paradox that attaches to the early novels of the 1890s: that, in proclaiming revolution, they inaugurate a long and extended counter-revolution against much that they had so vehemently and so triumphantly championed.

How this counter-revolution operated is hinted at in another of Thomas Mann's published remarks on Hamsun from 1929:

For him who has never known anything but what is palpably sound or palpably sick, there is something very bewildering indeed in the phenomenon of robust decadence and decadent robustness that Hamsun so enchantingly presents—and in the dualism, so organically reconciled, between the democratic modernity, the internationality, the highly developed refinement of his artistry and his aristocratic attachment to nature and the soil, from which there has derived everything that the world has had to suffer from him in the way of anti-social, anti-political, anti-literary, anti-democratic and anti-humanistic pontifications.

In spite of the intricate weave of these phrases, the warp and weft are traditional and familiar—content and style, or theme and technique, or (in a more contemporary idiom) poetry and belief. And it is necessary to recognize that Mann's pronouncement is less an explanation than a challenge: is there a formula that might account for this strange relationship in Hamsun between the 'how' and the 'what'? Unless one acts in some expectation of throwing light on the problem of the co-existence in Hamsun of these seemingly ill-matched qualities—the sophistication of his artistry and the bucolic conservatism of his later ideas—one abandons all hope of any solution to the central enigma there in favour of a beguiling but ultimately frustrating exercise in paraphrase.

It has been shown how the knowledge, the intuitions, the prognostications of the earliest heroes caught up in the game of life are fractional: living in that country that lies beyond commonplace ignorance and yet short of omniscient understanding, they enact an infinitely converging series that is forever approaching but never reaches the state of absolute certainty—like a series that says: 'To the half I know, I will by my ingenuity find out half of the remainder, and then again half the remainder, and then again half', with each term becoming more and more difficult to establish, and the sum total an ever more fearsome fraction. As for the beliefs that these novels serve, one remarks that they are for the greater part 'in character'; or to be more precise, are 'delivered ex-character'. It is true that the placing and the manipulation of these heroes helps to convey the idea that the individual is opposed to the mass, and that significant action is the consequence of personal endeavour and not of communal agreement; but the beliefs are made most explicit by the hero speaking his mind; for example, Nagel lets himself go on the subject of Tolstoi and Gladstone and all, and shocks the locals with his vaguely Nietzschean sentiments. These things are put there by a fairly crude act of insertion—it would not take much to convince one, for instance, that great chunks of Hamsun's famous lecture series of 1891 found their way without great modification into *Mysteries*, the author being content to use his created character as a mouthpiece. The beliefs and values in these early works are predominantly as the heroes say they are.

As one follows the novels in chronological order, one notices a number of apparently interrelated changes, and particularly that the technique they exploit and the attitude to life they communicate are in some kind of continuous and sensitive reciprocation. There is, for example, the question of where the author stations himself in his created world. In the early novels he is immanent; there is a very large measure of self-identification with these ultra-sensitive young men; the author is committed through them to the hectic game of life, and agrees for the purposes of his fiction to share their partial or fractional vision. In the novels of what might be called the author's middle-age—*Mothwise* (*Svœrmere*, 1904), *Under the Autumn Star* (*Under Høststjœrnen*, 1906), *Benoni* (1907), *Rosa* (1908), *With Muted*

Strings (*En Vandrer spiller med Sordin*, 1909) and *Look back on Happiness* (*Den sidste Glæde*, 1911)—there are grounds no less plausible for occasionally identifying the author with his own invented creatures, but the role he now plays is that of passive observer rather than active participant; the perspective itself is middle-aged, even elderly, the mood one of detachment, disengagement. And, to complete the trend, in the novels from 1913 onwards the withdrawal of the author, his alienation from his own world, is complete; he is no longer in his fictions except as a presence, there is contemplation from without, he has extricated himself from it all and now observes unobserved, sympathetically sometimes, sometimes sardonically.

As an accompaniment to this, the beliefs and attitudes sustaining these novels are less overtly inserted and more obliquely implied; what were in the world of *Mysteries* matters for vehement debate now tend to be written into the constitution; the ideas no longer invade but rather pervade the pages; they have to a very large extent ceased to be matters for question. Thus as the convictions harden over the years, the novels themselves perceptibly change their nature; they have ceased to be predominantly fictions about opiniated people, and instead they become imaginative demonstrations through fiction of a settled and on the whole pastoral (even feudal) scheme of values; anti-intellectual, anti-political, with a strong animus against commercialism, and an impatience with the pretentiously modern, they exhort by implication to a simple, decent probity, to a life of honest labour and a distrust of philosophizing, not unlike Candide's 'travailler sans raisonner'.

The changing perspective of the novels and the progressive hardening of the convictions they embody were matched by similar mutations in the way of life and the social attitudes of the author. Life, in the earliest days of his authorship was Oslo, Copenhagen, Paris; it was urgent correspondence with publishers, and organizing reviews of his books; it was meetings with editors and public lectures; it was at times a struggle for sheer physical survival—Hamsun incidentally was a most accomplished writer of begging letters, and it is said that in later life he would always respond sympathetically to any approach that was well-wrought and had the authentic touch. But simultaneously with the withdrawal of the author from his books went the withdrawal of the man himself from social competitiveness, the retreat to Northern Norway, the devotion to his estate, the desire to stand apart. When he now intervened in the debates of the day it was no longer with the exuberant intent of arguing or cajoling or shocking people, but rather as one who knew better —or simply one who knew.

But why should his views on life and social organization now be so aggressively simple? Why should they be what he had formerly scorned in others, views that were 'expressible in whole numbers'? The mathematical explanation of it is an appealing one. With the earlier infinite series that went on piling up ever more minute fractions, anything short of infinity left the sum total of understanding as an enormously complex fraction; but at infinity one remarks that such a sum plumps out into a figure simple and finite, and the practical intuitions are rounded out into—one. With a complete understanding of the ways of things, the kind of mental turmoil that was the defining sign of the early heroes would add up to certainty; or to put it in other words, at the point of ultimate omniscience, human complexity resolves itself into god-like simplicity. And there was after all one instance where this condition was fulfilled. To know all, to live in the certainty that nothing is concealed, to have all things ponderable and to have worked out the sum total of human folly, to be free from the ferment of doubt and the torment of partly knowing is not merely the prerogative of a god; it is also, if he so wishes, the privilege of the author within the fictional world of his own creating. And whilst it is always open to him to adopt for his own purposes the perspective of one of his own creatures, it is also within his power to act to this world as its god, as a remote omniscient being for whom the great fractional complexities of his characters' lives are reduced to simple, homely digits. One need not go so far as to assert that Hamsun ever consciously or deliberately claimed to have an omniscience in the real world equal to that which he elected to enjoy in the fictional one; but

that there was an affinity between the events of the two worlds
may, without extravagance, be suggested—that the inherent
superiority of the author here was matched by the authority of
one who felt himself inherently superior there.

It is against such a background of changing technique and
changing belief that *Growth of the Soil* (*Markens Grøde*, 1917)
must be seen. The novels that bracket it—*Children of the Age*
(*Børn av Tiden*, 1913) and *Segelfoss Town* (*Segelfoss By*, 1915)
from about the beginning of the First World War, and then from
1920 onwards *The Women at the Pump* (*Konerne ved Vandposten*,
1920), *Chapter the Last* (*Siste Kapitel*, 1923) and the August
books—*Vagabonds* (*Landstrykere*, 1927), *August* (1930) and *The
Road Leads On* (*Men Livet lever*, 1933), and finally *The Ring is
Closed* (*Ringen sluttet*, 1936)—record some of the futilities, the
synthetic inadequacies, the inauthenticities of modern life, offer-
ing a negative demonstration of belief. *Growth of the Soil* is,
however, the one real attempt to provide a positive exemplar,
the producible case, to make the ideal explicit. The result was
the most read, most translated, most praised and least characteristic novel that Hamsun ever wrote, and which by its almost
chance fame in being linked with the award of the Nobel Prize
has done more to misrepresent Hamsun (in England and America
at least) than anything else.

There was thus a time in the 1920s when appreciation of
Hamsun could be conducted in exclusively literary terms, when
a generous phrase could stand without any cautious scaffolding
of political disclaimer. When, however, Thomas Mann in 1951
made brief public reference to Hamsun, the change that had
taken place was at once evident. In the course of a B.B.C. talk
in honour of Bernard Shaw, Mann permitted himself an aside
that is interesting not merely for what it says but also for the
syntactical priorities it embodies: 'Still among us are the octo-
genarians André Gide, Shaw's kinsman in capricious genius and
protestant morality, and the aged Knut Hamsun, now merely
vegetating, a man broken by politics, though still the quondam
creator of highly discriminate narrative works.' The organization

of the sentence is such that the politics come first, and the authorship second. The pattern is one imposed by the times, a pattern which contemporary criticism neglects at the peril of being accused of suppressing material evidence; but just as it is imposed by the times, so time will surely change it.

Shaw and Hamsun were almost exact contemporaries; both were Nobel Prize winners; but it is about there that the resemblance ends. Shaw remained a single, fully articulated and consistently recognizable personality to the public; he created a *persona*, a quintessence of Shavianism, which he then lived up to. Hamsun, on the other hand, became to the European public at large two people, and his tragedy is our dilemma: how to reconcile, how to bring into focus the two public personalities he inhabited. By the 1930s people had begun to talk about him in the past tense; he was something one met in the histories of literature rather than in the book reviews, a row of collected works, a classic to be read in school, a phenomenon already classified and docketed by academic criticism. In 1940, however, he was again headline news, again in the centre of the stage, but this time playing not a literary part but a political one: at the age of eighty-one he threw his great influence on the side of the Nazis, played the role of Hitler's apologist, and earned for himself the contempt of his countrymen.

It is not the political or moral implications of this that are relevant here; only what helps to explain his work, namely that when, after 1945, life reached out and drew Hamsun down once again from his isolation into its immediacies and actualities, arraigned him in front of a tribunal, he countered this by imposing on the whole affair a fiction. For the regulation of his conduct, he adopted those principles that had sustained Nagel when he likewise was faced with the hostilities and menaces of life; he created a character with which he then identified himself, a character which first lived in the real world of the hospital at Grimstad, the Old People's Hostel at Landvik and the wards of the Psychiatric Clinic; and which then enjoyed a second life in the pages of his last book *On Overgrown Paths* (*Paa gjengrodde Stier*)—still not translated into English. One concrete example must suffice. It had been one of Nagel's stratagems, in his endless tussle with life, first to create and then later to destroy, and then again later still triumphantly to fulfil certain expectations concerning his own abilities—like the incidents, mentioned above, concerning the violin case containing dirty washing. The parallel with Hamsun's own war-time and post-war conduct is unmistakable. In 1940 he presented himself to the Norwegian people as one whose great age lent weight to his views, one who kept all his wits about him, and who had access to all the information; a leaflet circulated over his name, states: 'My age permits me to say something about the hideous confusion to which the last few days have brought us . . . I keep my eyes and ears open. I am not content with the babblings of short-sighted shipping magnates and Storting politicians. That is precisely why I read so many newspapers. . . . I have pondered both pro and contra.' Then in 1946, in the course of his evidence in court, he invited a wholly contrary interpretation of these same things:

And nobody told me that what I sat and wrote was wrong, nobody in the whole country. I sat alone in my room, entirely concerned with myself. I could not hear I was so deaf, nobody would have anything to do with me . . . . Everything had to be put to me in writing, and that became too much of a nuisance. I stayed sitting there. In these circumstances I could only go by my two newspapers, 'Aftenposten' and 'Frit Folk', and there was nothing in those two papers to say that it was wrong of me to sit and write.

At the end of the protracted investigation, he was—although of the real reasons one can still only speak speculatively—officially declared to be suffering from 'permanently enfeebled mental powers'. To this extent his fiction had succeeded; now everything was ready for the third part of the stratagem. Painfully, spelling out the pages in thick black strokes that he might follow what he had written, holding on with both hands to prevent the pencil from shaking, he wrote at the age of eighty-nine *On Overgrown Paths*, a brilliant evocation of a man living in bewildered ignorance, a work with passages of unimpaired vigour full of the authentic magic of his style. *On Overgrown Paths* is perhaps no novel, but it is magnificent fiction.

★ 11 ★

SIGRID UNDSET

In later years, Sigrid Undset clearly remembered the ink they used at school; it was dark blue with a dirty, sickly tinge, but it dried with a strangely metallic, coppery sheen. She used to draw pictures, a hut standing on a fjord, and make clouds by smudging the ink with her fingers. 'That gave such a mournful and impressive tone to her pictures', she wrote in reminiscence of the child that was herself, 'that she was quite touched by them. In reality she was by no means disposed to melancholy, but the peculiar blue tint of the school ink made it possible to produce gloomy landscapes without end.' Mournful, impressive, gloomy landscapes without end—these are the words by which she seems to have anticipated the summary judgements of the encyclopedias; for the traffic in gloom was something that Sigrid Undset seemed to carry over from her school days into her novels, there to create settings with the same metallic glint and the same impressively lowering atmosphere that the school ink had been so conducive to.

It is the endless and seemingly effortless stream of realistic detail that is the first conspicuous quality of her work. At bottom, it is the realism of a diagnostic report, drafted in great elaboration with the earnest purpose of assisting the individual to a greater awareness of himself, the whole then powerfully enriched by the concentrate of years of minute observation and dedicated historical study. Her exploration of the lower middle-class life of contemporary Oslo was based on ten years of preparatory routine clerical work (she was an office girl with an electrical firm in Oslo from 1899 to 1909); whilst her familiarity with Norway's history in the thirteenth and fourteenth centuries (the period of her two great historical novel cycles) was derived from the enthusiastic study natural to the daughter of a distinguished antiquary. Indeed the term 'realism', in its application to Sigrid Undset, is one of rich contradiction: the observed detail of her contemporary world, the grey and sombre setting for those characters whose longings are frustrated by routine work and financial cares, seems to possess all the poetic precision of an imaginative reconstruction; whilst the studied detail of the medieval works is shot through with all the vividness one might expect from an observer's report.

But all the apparently inexhaustible detail of 'landscape', of setting, of milieu, however integral it is to the purpose and direction of the novels, remains subsidiary to their moral purpose. It provides a background, it sets up a backcloth, it marks out an arena, against which and within which are performed a series of moralities. Each individual novel is disposed about a moral and religious axis in a fashion reminiscent of the way in which the whole corpus of Sigrid Undset's work is arranged about her year of decision—1924, the year of her conversion to the Roman Catholic faith. It is not merely that her decision was taken at very nearly the mid-point of her adult life; rather it is the astonishing way in which the one half of her work presents what is very nearly a mirror image of the other, with the fact of her conversion standing to the design of her life as a kind of axis of symmetry. Immediately to either side of it come the two first-magnitude, historical works, *Kristin Lavransdatter* (1920–1922) in three volumes, and *The Master of Hestviken* (*Olav Audunssön*, 1925–27) in four. Flanking these are the two groups of 'contemporary' narrative works: the three novels and four volumes of short stories she published between 1907 and 1918; and the four, rather more confessionally inspired, modern novels that belong preponderantly to the 'thirties. And ultimately, providing yet further reinforcement for the idea of symmetry, one remarks the two other historical 'outriders', stationed thirty years apart and equidistant from her conversion, *Gunnar's Daughter* (*Fortællingen om Viga-Ljot og Vigdis*, 1909), which is regularly but not altogether satisfactorily described as 'saga-

pastiche', and *Madame Dorthea* (1939), set in the Norway of
the 1790s.

Her life, to which this conversion acts as the great divide,
began its course under the powerful but benevolent interest of
her father, whom she greatly loved. The story of her childhood
up to the time of her father's death when she was eleven years
old is related with great sensitivity and a marvellously sure touch
in *The Longest Years* (*Elleve aar*, 1934). She was born in Denmark, on 20 May 1882, into a household where enthusiasm for
the past had a professional stamp and where the caution and
restrained scepticism such as is proper to the scholar was accepted
as a guiding principle. From the age of two she lived in Oslo,
in circumstances that steadily reduced as her father's illness
took the upper hand. When he died, she found herself in the
position that entraps so many of her own subsequent heroines:
that of belonging to a family with intellectual pretensions, of
coming from a cultured home that finds itself in straitened circumstances. After her school days proper, she attended the
Commercial High School, and in 1899 she took the office job
that held her for ten years until her royalties and a travelling
scholarship provided her with some measure of independence.
Already in these years, therefore, she combined in her own
person two things not commonly found in company, things
which nevertheless, separately and together, had a profound
effect on the direction her narrative talents took—a lively interest
in, and close familiarity with, the history of early Norway; and
an immediate, first-hand knowledge of the frustrated longings of
the lower middle-class.

Her first book to appear (an earlier one had been rejected and
then destroyed) was *Mrs. Martha Oulie* (*Fru Martha Oulie*,
1907), which was a novel in diary form; it was followed the next
year by *The Happy Age* (*Den lykkelige alder*), a collection of
rather shorter stories; both these books employ a contemporary
setting to examine the tensions set up between the secret dreams
and the drab realities of those who are caught up in the monotony
of everyday routine. It was not until 1911 that she enjoyed her
first popular success with *Jenny*, a novel which she wrote after a

visit to France and Italy; by its frank handling of certain erotic problems and its brutally realistic treatment of the unhappy love life of a woman artist, it stimulated much public debate. Another collection of short stories, *Poor Fortunes (Fattige skjæbner)*, appeared in 1912. There is a greater explicitness of emphasis in the moral tenor of her next novel, *Spring (Vaaren*, 1914). There is more than a hint of impatience with some of the more extreme 'liberal' and 'emancipated' ideas current in these years about women and their place in society; there is a re-insistence on woman's duties to her home and her children, and on the binding nature of her marriage vows—something of which one also finds in the later collections of stories, *Images in a Mirror* (*Splinten av troldspeilet*, 1917) and *The Wise Virgins (De kloge jomfruer*, 1918), as well as in the essay collection *A Woman's Point of View (Et kvindesynspunkt*, 1919). In these years, the material is drawn predominantly from her own immediate environment; her works treat contemporary matters, offer a detailed description of milieu, and are made with a penetrating and sometimes pitiless insight into human motives.

Up to this point her interest in the Middle Ages had been muted. There had been *Gunnar's Daughter* in 1909; and in 1915 she had composed her *Tales of King Arthur (Fortællinger om kong Arthur og ridderne av det runde bord)*—modest forerunners of the two works that filled the greater part of the 'twenties, *Kristin Lavransdatter* (which won for her the award of the Nobel Prize for Literature in 1928) and *The Master of Hestviken*. In 1925 her marriage to the painter A. C. Svarstad was annulled.

From then until the outbreak of war, Sigrid Undset once more turned to a preponderantly modern setting, with works that have a certain measure of Catholic tendentiousness: *The Wild Orchid (Gymnadenia*, 1929); *The Burning Bush (Den brændende busk*, 1930); *Ida Elisabeth* (1932) and *The Faithful Wife (Den trofaste hustru*, 1936), with the title of the last of her modern novels thus recalling in emphatic fashion the opening sentence of her very first: 'I have been unfaithful to my husband.' Three years later appeared her last novel, *Madame Dorthea*, set in Norway of the late eighteenth century. Apart from fiction, she wrote in these years a number of didactic, devotional, historical and critical pieces which were collected into *Catholic Propaganda* (*Katholsk propaganda*, 1927), *Stages on Life's Way* (*Etapper*, two vols., 1929, 1933), *St. Olav* (*Hellig Olav, Norges Konge*, 1930), *Saga of Saints* (*Norske Helgener*, 1937) and *Men, Women and Places* (*Selvportretter og landskapsbilleder*, 1938). When the Germans occupied Norway in 1940, she was forced to flee the country, her antagonism towards Nazism being traceable in things she wrote (some of them in German) as early as 1929. Travelling by way of Sweden and Russia, she managed to get to America, where she put herself at the disposal of the Norwegian information services. *Return to the Future* and *Happy Times in Norway* both appeared first in English in 1942. After the war she returned to Norway. She died on 10 June 1949. Posthumous publications include *Catharine of Siena* (*Caterina av Siena*, 1951) and *Articles and Speeches from the War* (*Artikler og taler fra krigstiden*, 1952).

The change from 'contemporary' to 'historical', the displacement of the action from the twentieth to the fourteenth century that came with *Kristin Lavransdatter* was essentially a technical change, on a par with the change in scale; the new trilogy was not in any essential sense an interruption or a digression in her career, and the characters in it, like those in her 'modern' works, are embodiments of a humanity and a human frailty that is timeless. The basic texture is the same; and if there seems at times a greater colourfulness in contrast to the earlier greyness, it is rather the lighting that has changed, and not the weave— like sackcloth illumined by stained glass. Some moments hint at the sagas, some of the linguistic elements of her style have a medievalism that is occasionally just a little indiscreet. But the realism is that of an author quite evidently much more at home in the chronicle than in, say, the *Novelle*. Her realism exploits the arrangement of mass detail rather than the economical selection of significant, and regards elaborateness itself as something inherent in life which, if subject to too severe a selective process, inevitably suffers distortion.

In Kristin's life there are four major upheavals, each one of which marks a critical point in the slow cyclical change of the generations, each introducing a new stage in the parabola-like progression from the peaceful serenity of a childhood home to the serene peace of a cloistered retirement, from the innocence of inexperience to the weariness of sated age. Between these two ultimates comes the relentless assault on the mind and the senses from the things of life, which (like the Town to the authoress as a child) is seen as a complex of fearsome attraction and sweet repulsiveness, of cruelty and compassion and suffering and joy, of traitorous loyalties and the infidelity of devotion. For *Kristin Lavransdatter* is upheld by the unshakable conviction of its author that purely monastic virtue is of little consequence, and that chastity counts for nothing in those who have never known the temptations of the flesh, nor goodness much cause for pride in those whose lives have remained insulated against evil.

The critical events for Kristin, broadly seen, are those in which her father, her husband and her sons implicate her, and which in their effect contribute to the formation of her personality and her maturity as a woman. The first comes when into her life of innocent piety (which is, however, sometimes menaced by bad dreams) there comes Erlend, who as her lover and subsequently as her husband brings unruly passion and disquiet and a guilty secret, who leads her over the frontier from maidenhood to womanhood and compels her to a re-appraisal of all that had seemed to her settled in its worth; her father, from being her protector, now becomes her new protector's antagonist, and her allegiances are put under review. The development from womanhood and wifehood to motherhood does more than introduce a new claim on her affection and loyalty; it forces upon her a new attitude to Erlend, whose role is now no longer merely that of lover and husband but also that of father to their children, of one who must provide security and stability and a disciplining example; and now she sees his inadequacy, sees how the gay irresponsibility that once made him so attractive now tells against him, and she realizes—to use the phrase Sigrid Undset once used elsewhere—that he is not the man whom she can regard

as her lord and master. It is this that introduces the most highly
developed and richly orchestrated section of the novel, with two
interwoven themes dominating: the search on the part of Kristin
for deeper insight into the stabler values of the church as,
hesitantly and uncertainly, she begins to pay more heed to its
teachings; and the history of a marriage so uncertainly poised.
Loving and nagging, attached to her husband yet ceaselessly
reproaching him for the dishonour he has brought her, devising
exquisite torment for him—playing the slut as a demonstration
of how low he has dragged her—yet fierce in her defence of him
against his enemies, Kristin lives in a bewilderment of alternating
surrender and resentment. Eventually he dies fighting in defence
of her honour, and Kristin, now at the head of the family, passes
on from the stage of simple motherhood to matriarchy. (That
Kristin should bear only male children, seven of them, is incidentally a matter to excite the psycho-analytical critic.) And
when finally her authority is past, when the sons' wives begin to
assert themselves, she accepts this new situation with its new
values; her duties and her functions as a woman are over, there
is no more for her to do as wife or mother, and she retires to a
nunnery.

The emphasis in the design of the novel rests on the relations
between individuals rather than on the qualities of the individuals
themselves; and there is built up a network of relationships in
which Kristin herself is the central and co-ordinating element.
In one respect the trilogy serves as a disquisition on woman's
loyalties: on the one hand, those which her menfolk impor-
tunately claim, her father, her husband and her sons; and on the
other, those absolute loyalties she owes to God. It traces the
consequences which this multi-dimensional conflict of claims
has upon her life, upon her standards of conduct, her sense of
integrity and self-respect; it considers how these claims often
merge with other factors, the calls of instinct and impulse and
desire, the dictates of will and conscience. It examines the nature
of the accessory phenomena of sin and guilt and remorse, making
a boldly patterned design, in which the pieces belong together
with all the digressionary consistency of an individual life. The

progression of the narrative through childhood and early maturity to adulthood, parenthood and age has the rhythm of organic growth, in which each moment has a significance and each stage a meaningfulness quite apart from its relevance to the ultimate design of things. Sigrid Undset is not concerned merely to complete her narrative pattern, but is intent on examining her theme at each stage in its development, and on demonstrating the consequential changes that occur in the total design with the advent of each new motif.

Additionally, there is an inexhaustible fascination in the subordinate detail; and Erlend, the husband, is a creation of genius. He, too, can be seen as the co-ordinating force in a private universe, holding together a complete though subsidiary system of cross-reference: between himself and Lavrans, son-in-law and father; or between himself and Simon, whereby the official fiancé who loses Kristin is matched against the illicit lover who wins her. And also some special mention must be reserved for the way Kristin is repeatedly positioned in her career by the sightings taken on Brother Edvin and Brother Gunnulf, the spokesmen of official religion, and on Fru Aashild, the personification of hedonism and religion's counterpole. And below it all, like a groundwork, is the insistence on the dominance over men's minds of the Church of Rome. In this, as well as in the very shape of the trilogy itself—starting with Kristin's first paternal loyalties, through the rebelliousness of adolescence and the bitter experience of adulthood to the final adoption of the Church's absolute values—there is a reflection and an anticipation of Sigrid Undset's own life.

Her conversion to Catholicism had a private significance, into which it would be impertinent to pry; but the mere fact of it nevertheless represents an item of evidence among others which all together point in the direction of a possible generalization: Sigrid Undset, like her heroines, betrays an interest in stability that is almost obsessive. Two things in particular helped, in the early days of her career, to make of her view of life a restless, oscillating instability. The first was her reluctance, fostered by her parents' training, to accept anything merely at its face value —like the things she was taught at school, or the authority of those who taught her. Her father, she later confessed, 'did what he could to sow distrust in her mind of the absolute value of what was taught at school, her mother took care . . . that Ingvild [i.e. Sigrid Undset] should not be overburdened with respect for her masters and mistresses in other directions'. This early hostility to 'received' opinion, this unwillingness to accept the truth of anything without close personal and sceptical scrutiny later became the chief ingredient of what it is usual to call the honesty of her vision. (It also seems, in her schooldays, to have marked her off and set her aside as 'precocious'.) But this doubting, questioning attitude was not confined to school, nor limited to her schooldays; and the insights, the flashes of revelation which this approach to things gave her into the motives underlying human conduct were both profoundly painful and also destructive of any firm basis of simple truth. At a very early age she was distressed by anything she felt to be affected, false or inauthentic, hating the recitation of poetry in class 'with feeling', resenting the mawkishness of *Little Women*, cringing under the parson's unctuous tones in the pulpit. She began to see through the deceptions we play on ourselves, realizing, for instance (she said), that the pomp and ceremony of burial is but a trick the living play on themselves to protect themselves against the terror of darkness and oblivion. And she tells also how oppressed she was by the secret she already as a child divined— 'that the sympathy one human being can give another is mixed up with sentimentality and self-gratification to such an extent as to make one loathe oneself—and then one makes the loathing an excuse for being unfeeling, and imagines that inhumanity is better than human frailty.' Pretence, of whatever degree of refinement or abstraction, she came to abhor: not merely the coarse-grained faults of hypocrisy where 'in our secret hearts' we know we act a lie; nor yet merely those instances of well-intentioned self-deception, where we unthinkingly adopt a manner, a tone, a gesture because the situation seems to demand it and not because it has its origins in our convictions; but embracing also those aspects of human affairs where we act in accordance with assumptions embedded deep and unscrutinized in the folds of our unconscious. A mind that follows this path—from the affirmation of human sympathy, via the detection of the apparent selfishness in the selflessness to its denial, and then back again via a realization of the heartlessness which this new attitude betokens to a re-affirmation of the original sympathy—is in a state of endless, restless oscillation. Left to itself, it hears only the menace of its own vibrating nerves; it feels the necessity for some stable and authoritative points of reference by which it can sustain its sense of direction. The first novels, not surprisingly, condemn by implication those ideas that supposed the individual to have no greater loyalty than to his own personal self; they insisted instead on those older and less modishly fashionable loyalties towards one's family, one's marriage partner, one's children and one's home.

But there was also, in her view of things, another (and, in part, complementary) unbalance that pervades the first group of 'contemporary' novels. In these, she is above all the interpreter of the Town. The town's fascination had the allurement of the forbidden, had all the lurking terror, all the excitement of being different; challengingly unexplored, it constituted a dangerous, attractive world of unwholesomeness and sin. Like the young hero of Hermann Hesse's *Demian*, she found herself as a child confronted with the need to reconcile this world with the world she had known at home, the world presided over by her father, with its decencies and sobrieties, its disciplined but gentle firmness, and its veneration of all that was open and upright; here was the world of the best parlour, of good conversation and fine books. And there was the maid's bedroom, with its whispered and ambiguous confidences and its cheap novelettes hidden among the underclothes in the bottom drawer but one in the chest. Sigrid Undset knew these paperback magazines: 'There was something in these romances which made one think of tainted water that had been forgotten in a carafe, of all the foul and unwholesome smells whereby the town became familiar to her senses. And they fascinated her in precisely the same way as

this quarter of the town where she now lived fascinated her. . . .'
She describes the fierce attraction Oslo had for her in these
years: the posters with their pictures of half-clad women, the
dubious literature in the seedy tobacconist shops, the hospital up
on the hill behind the church for people with dreadful diseases,
and the maternity ward and the girls who, as the maid said,
had had the bad luck to find themselves there. She heard tales
about the babies born there with deformities, of their being
bitten by rats, and she interpreted in her own way the silences
with which the maids met her pleas for more information.
'. . . In any case,' she wrote in *The Longest Years*, 'she learnt
from hints and covert speech that it was sufficiently illicit and
distressing and mysterious and uncanny to give her that complicated feeling of delight and horror which the town atmosphere
prompted her to look for in trying to extend her knowledge in
this direction.'

As a consequence of this, the defining characteristic of her
early heroines was an unstable equilibrium as they crossed and
re-crossed the frontiers of respectability and disrepute, living
between self-discipline and self-indulgence, between the obser-
vance of traditional decencies and the wilful pursuit of pleasure.
Furthermore, it was the tampering with this situation that seems
to make the later batch of 'contemporary' novels less of an
artistic than a devotional expression. Sigrid Undset's conversion
marked the completion of a process whereby her earlier scepticism of 'received' views found solace in the acceptance of dogma;
the meaning of *ex cathedra* took on a new significance for her
after her hostility to it in the context of school; or, to use what
might be a psycho-analyst's idiom, her reverence for her father
underwent mutation into reverence for the Father. The artistic
consequences were what D. H. Lawrence would not have hesitated to call 'immoral': 'Morality in the novel is the trembling
instability of the balance. When the novelist puts his thumb in
the scale, to pull down the balance to his own predilection, that
is immorality.' Equally, however, it is the persistence of the
earlier unbalance throughout nine-tenths of *Kristin Lavransdatter*
that makes the mediaevalism of it so massively incidental.

✳ 12 ✳

THE LITERATURE OF NYNORSK

In 1897, after eighty years of urgent and sometimes bitter controversy, Arne Garborg summed up the linguistic situation in Norway in a little book entitled *The Development of our Language* in phrases that even today go to the heart of the country's language problem:

We have not yet succeeded in creating an independent Norwegian literary language. Instead we have two languages. One of them is Norwegian, but is not yet a properly developed literary language; whilst the other is certainly a literary language but is not yet independently Norwegian. But now that the matters at issue have become clear, so also the task before us has been clarified. Quite clearly what must be striven for is some kind of combination of the two languages. The Norwegianness of the one must join the literary qualities of the other. Then we shall have reached our objective.

Certainly, of all the problems that confronted Norway after winning her independence in 1814, the language problem has shown itself to be the most persistent; and Garborg's summary of the situation clearly reflects the diabolical simplicity of the initial situation: Norway's official and written language in 1814 was Danish, introduced as a governmental language in those centuries when Copenhagen was supreme, and used in the country's administration, in its churches, its courts and its schools; the common speech of its people was, however, the sum of a number of vernacular dialects that were genuinely Norwegian enough to satisfy national pride, yet which had no written norm. The problem of reconciling these two conflicting elements is one that has bedevilled the intellectual life of Norway ever since; the debate if anything increases in bitterness (and, as some maintain, in absurdity) as the years pass; yet the seeming comedy of a small nation of less than four million inhabitants permitting itself the extravagance of two languages, neither of which in contrast with the languages of Switzerland has any currency outside her own frontiers, is laughable only to those who overlook the deeper tragedy of it all—the saddening spectacle of a small nation irrevocably hardening into two separate factions whose disputes feed party political strife and set off town against country, and where even honest and scrupulous negotiations seem so distressingly easily to degenerate into strident propaganda.

Inevitably almost, one scrutinizes Wergeland first in looking for the origins of the strife; and it is wholly characteristic that one discovers both sides claiming support for their policies in him. It is true that he had things to say about this matter, as he had about most; he was greatly attracted by the idea that a story told in the language of Hardanger or Sogn or Trøndelag might be shown to embody stylistic elements that derived from the language of the sagas; he was inclined to respond to language as a mystic force that established some kind of divinely authorized national frontier; and he gave it as his conviction that one of the main signs of a people's independence (and also a lasting guarantee for it) was an indigenous literature written in a native medium; his anxiety to do something about this problem was, in other words, as much by way of defence against any future cultural aggression from Sweden as it was a reaction against Denmark.

Two complementary policies developed, and found expression about the middle of the century in the work of two men, themselves almost exact contemporaries. The one was Knud Knudsen, whose approach was to attempt a 'purification' of the existing written language, to promote the use of certain selected words of a more specifically Norwegian character in place of the existing Danish ones, to adapt the written norm to conform more to the Norwegian mode of pronunciation, and to urge an orthography that reflected the more vigorous treatment of consonants than was awarded them in Danish. The approach prospered, and has since stimulated a number of official reforms that have had as their object the closer approximation of the spelling to Norwegian speech habits. The other movement was more radical, seeking to create on the basis of the various regional dialects a synthetic language which nevertheless would emphasize the links that bound the modern speech with its Old Norse sources; in this the initiative came mainly from Ivar Aasen. The history of this movement is one of ceaseless pressure to get *Landsmål* (or, as it subsequently came to be known, *Nynorsk*) officially recognized and accepted and used, and to insist that it be given equal right with the existing written language (*Riksmål*, later called *Bokmål*) as an authorized medium of communication. The efforts in this direction, which since 1906 have been co-ordinated by the body known as 'Noregs Mållag', have met with considerable political success; already before the turn of the century, *Landsmål* had become a compulsory subject at all teacher training colleges, schools were allowed to decide for themselves which of the two languages was to be used as the medium of instruction, and a chair in the subject was created at the University of Oslo; new and important concessions were later won concerning the use of *Nynorsk* in the church, in the courts, in the armed forces, in university examinations, in the post office, in local government and on the state railways.

Had this been all, however, the language would have remained simply and obstinately synthetic, emphasizing the incipient weakness of the whole movement: that although the language was indeed based on what was spoken, yet nobody spoke precisely it. The language needed using, needed exercising, needed its innate power developing and rehearsing and ultimately applied to literary objectives; it needed to parade itself and its potentialities. And in the emergence of *Nynorsk* as a literary medium, three names at least call for mention: Arne Garborg who first displayed its poetic capabilities; Olav Duun who exploited its terse eloquence; and Tarjei Vesaas who is its greatest stylist.

Among the factors that exerted a formative influence on Arne Garborg, three in particular catch the eye. The first was that he lacked what practically every other Norwegian author possesses in high degree—an affection for his own native district. He was born on 25 January 1851 in that strange, almost uncanny, region to the south of Stavanger known as Jæren, a flat or at most gently undulating, treeless district with broad sand-banks and shifting sands, shallow bays, and small forlorn farms in a setting of moorland bog, all so un-Norwegian in its mood and character. From these sad and silent wastes, Garborg escaped with a sense of release, and seemingly without any feelings of disloyalty: 'Uglier and uglier it appeared to me the older I became. And without the least sigh, I left it.' But it left him without any permanent anchorage, and was one of the several elements that contributed to the general feeling of homelessness and rootlessness he suffered from in later life. Then there was the gloom and oppressiveness of his childhood; when the young Garborg was nine, his father fell prey to hypochondria and religious mania, and the boy was subjected to stern domestic discipline in a household suddenly strictly Pietist; his reading was in large measure restricted to the Bible, he was discouraged from playing his childhood games, and for a time was not even permitted to attend school. His relationship with his father grew into a complex and tormenting one; and when in 1870 his father committed suicide, the nineteen-year-old Garborg suffered a hurt that never quite healed. Thirdly, and linked with both the above considerations, was the fact that Garborg was *odelsgut*, i.e. the eldest son whom both tradition and the law exert pressure on to take over the family land and work it; these obligations Garborg denied, and instead gave himself over to literature and intellectual pursuits. Thus it was only by abandoning his homeland, by (as it seemed to him) driving his father to his death, and by neglecting his family duty that Garborg cleared a way for himself as a writer; the residual sense of guilt that remained clouds his work, hanging there like a suspension and giving it its peculiar acrid flavour.

After his literary début in 1873 he passed through many enthusiasms, experimented in many styles, and contributed to many controversies—indeed in some instances he was the controversy, when for instance he applied for a government scholarship and was refused for reasons that were moral and political rather than artistic. He began with romantic inclinations, which in the early 1870s gave way to a consuming admiration for Ibsen (and especially the Ibsen of *Brand*). In the late 1870s and in the 1880s he made his mark essentially as a prose writer, displaying an untiring interest in the debates of the day—the religious conflicts that came with the clash of positivism, pietism and Grundtvigianism, the so-called 'morality debates' that centred round the publication of Hans Jæger's *From Christiania's Bohemia* (*Fra Kristiania-Bohêmen*, 1885) and the controversy that turned on the threat to the rural way of life from modern urban culture. His first novel *A Freethinker* (*Ein Fritenkjar*) began to appear as a serial in 1878 and was published in book form in 1881; and in 1883 he brought out *Students from the Country* (*Bondestudentar*) —'that profound and serious book about Norway's poverty', as Brandes called it—which is perhaps the best novel in the style of Naturalism to have been written in Norwegian; and in 1886 he wrote *Men* (*Mannfolk*), in which he attacked the prevailing conventional ideas on sex and which marked his contribution to the 'Bohemia' debates.

About the year 1890, at a time when he suffered from acute financial difficulties and also seemed unable to find any firm basis for his own personal philosophy, his fortunes appeared to be at their lowest ebb. It was at this time that he dabbled in many things, anarchism, Buddhism, Nietzscheanism, spiritualism— things of which his novel *Weary Men* (*Trætte Mænd*, 1891) with its emphasis on the meaninglessness and purposelessness of life was the precipitation. In 1890, however, his novel *At Mother's* (*Hjaa ho Mor*) won a German literary prize, and there followed a change for the better in his fortunes. In the decade which followed, in addition to *Weary Men* which was perhaps his greatest popular success, he also wrote a novel *Peace* (*Fred*, 1892), his poem cycle *Haugtussa* (1895), which is his finest work, and the drama *The Teacher* (*Læraren*, 1896), in which he embodied many of his own personal views.

Many of the things he wrote later combine to define his maturer philosophy of life: *The Lost Father* (*Den burtkomne Faderen*, 1899), a prose poem in diary form; *Jesus Messiah* (*Jesus Messias*, 1906), a statement of his own liberal theology, and *The Lost Messiah* (*Den burtkomne Messias*, 1907) which is a rejoinder to those who criticized it; and *The Son Returned* (*Heimkomin Son*, 1908). These all belong in essence to the attempt to define what Garborg felt the message of Jesus had really been—an appeal to brotherhood and love. To these years belongs also *In Helheim* (*I Helheim*, 1901), which formed a continuation to *Haugtussa*, and the autobiographical *Letters from Knudaheio* (*Knudaheibrev*, 1904). His last years were devoted to translation, which he regarded as part of the necessary training and discipline for a language and a test of its stamina and range. He died on 14 January 1924.

Garborg is one of those writers of whom it comes more naturally to speak of 'the services' they have rendered to literature and to human affairs than of their achievements in them. In this he is perhaps comparable with Bjørnson, a comparison that gains unexpected force precisely from the very dissimilar nature of the two men, Garborg being a small, quiet man, with an inturned temperament, a penetrating and analytical mind that delighted in problems, and an intellect that burned with a hard bright flame. He was unusually versatile: a novelist of power, an occasional dramatist, a lyric poet of haunting quality in the exquisite *Haugtussa*, a translator of Shakespeare and of Goethe's *Faust* and of the *Odyssey*. Above all, however, it was Garborg's genius for being implicated in things that made him, in the last decades of the nineteenth century particularly, the Norwegian equivalent of what Lessing had been to eighteenth-century Germany: a crucible into which the ideas of the time were cast and made to give a purer yield. Garborg's own image of himself was of one who pointed out the way:

> Yes that was surely the purpose of my life:
> that bitter experience
> should make of me a teacher for others
> and one who points the way.

Nobody who seeks to understand the controversies and the cross-currents of this most difficult age for Norway can afford to pass over Garborg, or to neglect what he said and wrote and stood for.

Over certain areas of the Norwegian novel, regionalism sits like an encrustation, a thick barnacling of local detail on a structure often too insubstantial to carry it; to this, the novels of Olav Duun form an honourable and impressive exception. It is true they belong inseparably to the district their author was born into: Namdal, and the Namsen Fjord, lying about a hundred miles north of Trondheim, between that city and the Lofotens; but what they derive from the locality is present not as an accretion but as an assimilation, an ingestation even, something that has entered into them to fuel them and drive them on. Duun was a late beginner, and slow to mature. Born on 21 November 1876, he spent his early manhood up to the age of twenty-four in the way young men of a *bonde* family were expected to spend it, working the land in the summer, fishing in the winter. In 1901 he began a course at a teacher training college, where a shrewd and intelligent tutor encouraged his desire to write and shape his talents. His first book, a volume of short stories, did not appear until he was over thirty, in 1907; his greatest achievement, the six-volume novel *The People of Juvik* (*Juvikfolke*) belongs to his mid-forties. He died at the age of sixty-two in 1939.

It is tempting to think of the things Duun wrote before 1918 as separate and even planned preliminary studies, as tentative investigations of those themes and ideas that go to make up *The People of Juvik*: studies in the kinds of character that take ultimate form as Odin and Lauris; explorations into the workings of an awakening Christian conscience and a sense of social responsibility in a world where many of the old heathen virtues were still awarded approving recognition; analyses of what was assertive in man and what submissive, of moods of confidence and feelings of inferiority and the mechanism of their reactions in a changing world. These early works insist that life is a matter in which the individual has to assert himself, a battle to be fought, a never-ending conflict with one's fellows, with the compulsions of society and convention and with the invisible powers that flicker and play about our earthly existence. It is a battle which, when the world's hostility meets suspected or discovered weakness, the individual must fight defensively and with sickened grimness; but which, where the man is strong and favourably endowed for our combative existence, is waged with an eager and an intense joy. The young hero of the first short novel *Marianne* (*Marjane*, 1908) is one of those on the defensive—a young boy who has to face the reaction of the world about him to the fact of his shameful home background, with his slut of a mother and his thieving father. More explicitly in *Crosswise* (*Paa Tvert*, 1909), the hero Danel is literally crippled at the outset; and because he trains himself to meet the world's unthinking cruelty towards him with a hard and unyielding bitterness and a determination to be in some way revenged on life, he sustains himself. Only one thing is he defenceless against, and that is pity; with the result that he deliberately sets out to provoke the hostility of others, for only thus can he find a source of strength that will allow him to manage things on his own. A later variation on the same theme is *Harald* (1915), in which the hero is essentially well-equipped to meet life's challenge but who, because there is no one class of society in which he feels instinctively at home, revenges himself on all by deliberately seeking to antagonize; only by his innate resourcefulness and courage does he eventually succeed in winning the sympathy of others. In *Hilderøya* (1912), Duun traces the reaction of one whose contentment is upset by the appearance of a newcomer to the district who, by the mere fact of his presence, constitutes a challenge to which the hero is compelled by his innate sense of inferiority to respond; and in seeking ways of demonstrating his superiority over the stranger, he acts senselessly, recklessly, and generally to his own disadvantage. In *Three Friends* (*Tre venner*, 1914) Duun examines the dynamics of a triangle of forces that links three friends, tensions that both hold them to each other and yet at the same time keep them apart.

In all these novels, the impressive thing is the acuteness of the psychological portrayal, the exploration of human motives and reactions in conditions of stress—it is relevant that Duun admitted that Dostoevski had meant much to him. In *The Good Conscience* (*Det gode samvite*, 1916), however, there came a more extended treatment of something which, whilst not actually lacking in Duun's earlier work, only later and especially in the opening volumes of *The People of Juvik* was to provide one of the main sources of his narrative power: the loyalty to family tradition and to inherited land. This, and the conflict between it and conscience as it shows itself in three separate generations, is the framework about which this novel is built. First of the generations is that of the man little troubled by conscience, or even by thought of ultimate retribution, when it is a matter of preserving the family land; but then his son, however much he tries to deny the demands of conscience—'Conscience,' he says, 'I've hung that up on the wall. Finished with it'—is less inspired by the older spirit of things that meant so much to his father, and is consequently much more vulnerable to the assault of conscience in the long run; the representative of the third generation, the daughter, is finally one who comes to a kind of recognition that conscience does indeed make cowards of us all; she by a deliberate act of will leads her life accordingly, with a conscious adoption of the traditions of the *ætte*—the family line or tradition, the interests of the clan—as the standard by which to measure her actions. The last of this group of novels *On Lyngsøya* (*Paa Lyngsøya*, 1917) returns temporarily to a predominantly psychological theme. It follows the career of one who is led to the conviction that he has somehow been 'chosen' to 'suffer': one who finds an inverted pleasure in cherishing his sexual frustrations, who deliberately invites the suspicions of others that he is to blame for certain acts of violence in the district, and who delights in the opportunity for martyrdom. The successive spiritual crises of this twisted mind are investigated with an impressive skill and insight.

The novels of these years up to the First World War are far from being free of artistic error, especially when it is a question of stressing or clarifying the ethical content; the 'message' sometimes only too evidently dictates the course of the action, or else obtrudes too directly or too explicitly in the speech of those involved. In particular Duun seems to proclaim too blatantly his antagonism towards 'the chapel'. One of the essays he wrote whilst at the teacher training college—an essay which is claimed to present in embryonic form many of the dominant ideas of his subsequent work—bore the revealing title of 'God Helps Those Who Help Themselves'. His old-time heroes, those who draw their strength from their awareness of belonging to a family tradition, are too arrogant to pray, too proud to beg for God's help in time of trouble, feeling that their self-respect demands of them that they carry things through alone or not at all. They regard the Almighty as somebody open to approach on a contractual basis; somebody of whom certain things might possibly be asked but only in exchange for so much good behaviour; somebody to whom, if one abstains from asking in the first place, one is not beholden in any way. These novels in the aggregate carry the suggestion that such proud and arrogant self-sufficiency had been one of the chief factors in sustaining the Norsemen, both of past centuries and of the present day, in the battle for life—something that the meekness and humility of chapel teaching was directly undermining.

The six volumes of *The People of Juvik* appeared in successive years, between 1918 and 1923: *The Trough of the Wave* (*Juvikingar*, 1918); *The Blind Man* (*I blinda*, 1919); *The Big Wedding* (*Storbryllope*, 1920); *Odin in Fairy Land* (*I eventyre*, 1921); *Odin Grows Up* (*I ungdommen*, 1922); *The Storm* (*I stormen*, 1923). The narrative proper begins at the end of the eighteenth century and runs through the beginning of the twentieth, it is *par excellence*, the novel of the *ætte*, the traditionally Norse concept of the family or clan or unit of kin, and its role and significance; in this work the author examines the primitive form of society on which modern rural Norwegian life has been based, examines its assumptions, its attitudes to God and to Nature, and traces its decline through its more modern manifestations and into the present century. It surveys the changing pattern of impulse and endeavour through that very critical century in Norway's development, the nineteenth; it shows the impact of new loyalties upon the old, the widening of the horizons from personal and clan interests through to those of local community and eventually of nation; it examines the inevitable decadence that follows in those cases where the old standards crumble away and no new thing is found adequate to replace them, where all sense of purpose disappears, where introversion and introspection are the symptoms of a new and ominous sickness of the age. (This is perhaps also another way of saying that, like so much else in European literature at this time, it betrays the impact which the First World War made on a generation only too aware that things had irrevocably changed and were still changing.)

The culmination of *The People of Juvik* is, however, undoubtedly to be found in the creation of the character (and symbol) of Odin, and the crux of the conflict lies in his changing relations through the three final volumes with his adversary Lauris. It has been suggested that the first three volumes, which chronicle a century's history of the family Odin belongs to and define its traditions, are really an account of the collective unconscious to which Odin is heir. Duun's own attitude to his character is revealed in a letter he wrote in January 1921: 'Now the struggle is on: to create the man of "restitution"—he who in his own life must pass through everything his forefathers managed to stagger through, and then gain a further advance of "one chicken's pace".' The six books represent a highly disciplined and deftly controlled piece of artistry, sure in its composition and richly motivated.

Each volume has its own tone . . . [wrote Arnulf Øverland]. The first volume is a saga, the technique of which consists as far as possible in merely reporting the outward events and letting the characters stand out in the light of them. The second volume . . . is rather broader and has the tone of a heroic epic. In *The Big Wedding* there is more weight placed on the descriptions of the district and its people, it is multicoloured and gay, a scherzo. *Odin in Fairy Land* is an idyll, yet simultaneously it is a very serious description of the world of a child. The last two volumes are contemporary novels, where two types of individual and two social philosophies fight a battle to the death. Yet the unity of the work is nevertheless in good order; it is a progressively advancing 'family' history, the line of which is clear: the Norwegian on his way into the twentieth century.

The novels that followed *The People of Juvik* often seem to be functioning as a kind of additional commentary to particular aspects of it, a filling out or a refining of those things whose subtleties or profundities provided an endless challenge and stimulation to the author. A few years after the completion of this large-scale work, he attempted another big narrative—not quite so extensive in its design, but originating in the same problem that had formed the final dilemma that faced Odin: what are the arguments for combating evil with evil, and may one kill to save innocence from villainy? The moral ramifications of this and the network of relationships between people exposed to this problem and affected by it, are traced out in the trilogy of consisting of *Fellow-beings* (*Medmenneske*, 1929), *Ragnhild* (1931) and *Years of Old Age* (*Siste Leveåre*, 1933). In 1936 there appeared the novel *The Present Age* (*Samtid*), and two years after that he published the novel, the title of which many have been quick to seize on as defining the real object of Duun's exploratory authorship: *Man and the Powers* (*Menneske og maktene*). Here is probably the supreme example in Duun's work of something which is ineluctably Norwegian and yet archetypal in design, based on a timeless pattern, yet worked in local materials. It tells of an isolated community living on a small island which (according to legend) is destined at some time or another to be swallowed up by the sea, and when it seems that this very danger is in fact being threatened, when the level of the sea begins to rise, there is exerted on the souls of those living there an intense pressure. The novel, in following what happens to individual loves and hates, and joys and fears when they are threatened by a common peril, seems to make unambiguous reference forward to the war that was less than a year away.

The truth of the psychological revelation in Duun's work is one of the sources of its great strength; and where it is a question of uncovering the secret motives of the pretentious and loud-mouthed—especially the nationalistic and religiously loud-mouthed—he can be quite pitiless. His characters have that quality loosely described as 'depth', carrying with them an air of unsuspected possibilities and potentialities; they never merely 'stand for' something or other, and even the most minor of them are never merely representative of an attitude or a policy or a way of life but give the impression of genuinely rounded personalities, complete with all the surprisingly unexpected and yet genuinely consistent quirks of behaviour and unreason that make them individuals. But Duun's analysis does not stop there, indeed this seems in many ways to be for him only a starting-point; for what he obviously found of absorbing interest was the interaction of personality, the interpenetration of individual motives and urges, the pattern of forces that builds up when two or three or four people are brought together by circumstance, the mysterious and seemingly incompatible or conflicting emotions and tensions that are set up between brother and brother, between children and parents, between man and woman, between lovers and between friends and between those who are brought into intimacy by mutual hate, in the endless fascination of attraction and repulsion and imposed adjustment.

The spatial reality of this fictional world is extremely limited. Beyond the valley, outside the fjord, one realizes that there must be governments conspiring, armies moving, statesmen conferring; yet these things make little obvious impact on the world in which Duun's characters live—quite unlike the way in which Sigrid Undset's mediaeval world, for instance, reverberates with the clash of events from the world outside. On those rare occasions when Duun does attempt to position this restricted and remote and very nearly self-sufficient world within a wider context of dynastic and political change, the device operates in a rather pathetic way, like an obtrusive footnote of historical reference:

It was Jens who came in. Quickly Valborg got up; she could hardly stand the sight of him now. More ill-mannered than ever, he began: 'You know Valborg, we are under the Swedes now, I've just been talking to the Sheriff himself. It's quite clear: yon Karl Johan is King of

Frederikstein and the whole of Norway, eh? He can go to the devil,
I say.

The People of Juvik.

Yet although historical event and incident act only as a very
loose framework of reference in these works, the narrative is
nevertheless carefully and firmly integrated with the profounder
shifts and movements of human endeavour. Duun's sensitivity
was that of a seismograph, a sensitivity which ignores the more
conspicuous trafficking of immediate event and detects behind
it all the deeper and more distant shifts that affect the founda-
tions of our existence; this is the gift that allows him to record
with rare delicacy, even in a remote milieu, the profounder
changes in human attitude and belief that ripple through the
world unnoticed and unsuspected by more superficial observers.
More than anything else, it is this quality that preserves his work
from being merely parochial. It is true that his work is firmly
rooted in Namdal; the Norwegian-ness of it is deeply felt, but
it is conveyed without the slightest trace of sentimentality. He
has a level view of this, just as he had also of Nature, which is
never anything to rhapsodize over, or even to exploit as an
objectivication of mood, nor even to serve as a fascinating background; Nature is something his characters are seen not against
but in, something it would be unthinkable to have them separate
from. Duun never fell prey, as so many *Heimatdichter* have done,
to the temptation of describing what was merely or picturesquely
regional in the way of costume, habit, food or local arrangement:
his regionalism has all the universality of Hardy's.

Tarjei Vesaas was born on 20 August 1897, and he was fortunate in possessing in high degree what Garborg so tragically
lacked: a quiet affection for his native district of West Telemark,
which incidentally is one of the richest in folk poetry in the
whole country. Apart from a period as a very young man at the
Folk High School at Voss, and a number of visits abroad in later
years, he has spent all his days in the region he was born in,
matching his way of life to his temperament, withdrawn and

reserved, and content to live by the deliberate and regular tempo of the countryside. But it would be a great mistake to assume that this way of life betokened a kind of intellectual isolationism; not only was he more than usually receptive to the influence of other writers—Kipling, for example, meant much to him in his early days, and Hamsun and Selma Lagerlöf and Kinck—but, as his war-time novels published during and immediately after the Occupation testify, he was also extremely sensitive to the undertones accompanying the march of events and to the response of his people; few authors have listened so attentively to the complex jangling melodies of modern life, or given so penetrating, if oblique, an analysis of it. Domestic opinion puts him with Pär Lagerkvist and also alongside Kafka, yet with a significant distinction: 'One is reminded', wrote Sigurd Hoel, 'of the difference between the Old and the New Testament. In Tarjei Vesaas, there is so much more *hope*—and a gentler note.'

From the point of view of style, Vesaas's work from his début at the age of twenty-six with a short novel entitled *Children of Men* (*Menneskebonn*, 1923) up to the present day offers the record of one who has sought unremittingly to discipline his style. He made his mistakes early, and profited by them; his first novel was refused by the publishers and was thrown on the fire, presumably along with some of the bad habits that had contributed to it; nor was it his only rejection in these early years. But the year after his début, he published *Messenger Huskuld* (*Sendemand Huskuld*, 1924), a novel which, in spite of its digressiveness and sentimentality, was not without power to move. The adverse criticism that greeted his next three works (two dramas and a novel) perhaps convinced him that some things might be written too easily, for his next work did not appear until 1928, a novel *The Black Horses* (*Dei svarte hestane*), where the tighter control over the composition and the language is at once apparent. It is only now, however, at this distance in time, that one can see not merely that this was the beginning of a process, but also *how* it was; how it was a *point de départ* in the sense that the road Vesaas subsequently followed meant a steady departure from the realistic style it affected rather than a following up; it was, as it were, an exercise that required to be completed before the author could move on. From this point he followed a quest for new ways of adding to the allusiveness and suggestiveness of his words without destroying (and indeed where possible enhancing) the terse economy of his methods; his task was to fine everything down in the greatest possible degree, to increase the efficiency of his communication in a kind of engineering sense by improving the power-to-weight ratio, by giving it a super-charged power of intimation and cutting away everything superfluous; the result was to combine strength and lightness in a way reminiscent of some of the best of modern architecture, to give an audacity of range to his seemingly frail constructions that is altogether amazing.

His work in the 'thirties is dominated by two separate but chronologically overlapping groups of novels: the one, a group of four novels dealing with the career of Klas Dyregodt, is made up of *Father's Journey* (*Fars reise*, 1930), *Sigrid Stallbrokk* (1931), *The Unknown Men* (*Dei ukjende mennene*, 1932) and, several years later, *The Heart Hears Songs of Home* (*Hjarta høyrer sine heimlandstonar*, 1938); the other group, with Per Bufast as its central figure, consists of the two novels *The Great Game* (*Det store spelet*, 1934) and *Women Calling Home* (*Kvinnor ropar heim*, 1935). It is to these two groups of novels, and to the development that is visible in them, that Sigrid Undset's remarks of 1947 most particularly apply:

One remarked his peculiarly lyrical style, the power he had of creating his own world—a narrow and closed world perhaps, where the people suffer hurt because they take themselves so distressingly seriously and are inclined to see other people only as supporting characters in the drama of their own lives. Until, that is, he wrote himself free of this cloddish world with his 'Bufast' books, that fine picture of a little, closed world which is, however, not narrow because all the people on the estate know they are so dependent on each other, so that they all live more than just their own lives.

And already here there is a hint of what has in time come to be recognized as the current ethical theme traceable in and through so much of Vesaas's work, above all in his works of the 'thirties: the theme of the 'helping hand' offered, sometimes unknowingly and sometimes deliberately, to a man who has reached the very flash-point of despair, and the inscrutable ways whereby a whole personal destiny can be changed by a readiness (or sometimes no more than a hint of readiness) to make sacrifices for others. Thus alone, he suggests, can man sustain himself and others in a world of disintegration and dread and hidden menace.

Separate from these two groups of novels, and with its own idiosyncratic quality, is *The Sandalwood Tree* (*Sandeltreet*, 1933), a novel based on the situation where a woman, who already has two children aged eleven and twelve, finds herself pregnant for the third time and knows by a kind of presentiment that she will die in childbirth; she feels a great desire to see something of the wider world before she dies, and her husband sells all their possessions that they may set out and travel through Norway, by sea, road and rail, and eventually on foot; but the device that lends distinction to the work is that the world which the woman so deliberately sets out to see and to experience is viewed not exclusively through her eyes but also—by a decision of genius—through the eyes of the two children living under the pressure of their changed circumstances.

A change came with the war, a turning-point where the technical progress in his art followed naturally upon what had been achieved in the previous decade, but where the direction changed. Allegory in the service of mysticism, the symbol as the weapon of the visionary, these are the things of which the novels of the latest years give testimony: *The Seed* (*Kimen*, 1940), *The House in the Dark* (*Huset i mørkret*, 1945), *The Bleaching Ground* (*Bleikeplassen*, 1946), *The Tower* (*Tårnet*, 1948), *The Signal* (*Signalet*, 1950), *Spring Night* (*Vårnatt*, 1954) and *The Birds* (*Fuglane*, 1957). *The Seed* appeared in the first autumn of the Occupation, *The House in the Dark* in the autumn immediately following the end of the war; and each of them in an oblique but intimate way expressed something of the deeper feeling of these years. One must understand that just as, shall one say, the Inflation was to one generation of Europe, or the Depression to

another, or the War, so the Occupation was to a whole generation of Norwegians an ordeal of a very special and testing kind,
a regional mutation of war's hideousness. That it should inspire
the country's artists and writers was natural and inevitable; that
it should encourage such excessively literal and repetitive treatment as one finds for example in the mural paintings of Oslo
Town Hall is unfortunate; but here in Vesaas it is the very lack
of realism that makes everything so real, there being no report
of what took place but instead a reconstruction of how it was—
the first of these two novels demonstrating in its indirect way the
spread of evil passion through a community, and the second of
them in its superbly fantastic way taking in the whole atmosphere
of the domestic war years under the roof of its capacious and
intricately contrived symbol. The novels of the war and of the
post-war years explore the nature of decay and sickness and
frustration as the earlier ones had that of the living and the vital;
and with *The Bleaching Ground* Vesaas produced one of the most
remarkable novels of the present age.

Vesaas is primarily a novelist and short story writer, but not
exclusively. In 1946 he published his first volume of lyric poetry
The Springs (*Kjeldene*), which he has followed up with three
other volumes of verse. Of his ability as a dramatist, opinion in
his own country is still uncertain; but it is of some interest that
in recent years Vesaas has given careful attention to the technical
demands of the radio play, and several pieces by him written
specially in his idiom have been broadcast since the war. It is,
however, as a narrative writer that his chief contribution has
been made to Norwegian literature, and upon which his international reputation is basing itself. A collection of short stories
under the title *The Winds* (*Vindane*, 1952) won first prize in an
international competition in Venice, since when it has been
translated into French, German, Italian, Danish and Swedish;
it was of one of these stories that a prominent Swedish critic
wrote that, beside it, the treatment of children one finds in
Katharine Mansfield and Rosamund Lehmann seemed pale and
'literary'. Other of his works have been translated into German,
Danish, Swedish, Czech, Dutch, Finnish and Latvian. To his

loss, and to our greater shame, his work is today unknown in either England or America.

Garborg's services to *Nynorsk*, which were of course as much those of the apologist as those of the practitioner, require to be judged in the wider context of his defence of the *bonde* against the economic aggression from capitalism and the cultural infiltration from the towns. He reacted firmly against Bjørnson's insinuations that 'culture' was the monopoly of *Riksmål* and vigorously counter-claimed that not only had the *bonde* been the real custodian of Norwegian culture during the time of his country's subservience to Denmark, but also that in the last resort his language was superior to *Riksmål* in its literary potentialities. But the example of both Duun and Vesaas illustrates the dilemma that faces a writer who selects *Nynorsk* as his vehicle. On the one hand there is the obvious and considerable advantage of disposing over an unspoilt medium, with all the exciting possibilities of creating, out of a language as yet untainted by bureaucratic usage, a unique instrument for his imaginative purposes. He enjoys a freer hand, he can more easily mould things to his own personal style, and by exploiting all the latent qualities of a new material succeed in saying things never said before. What he cannot do, however, is have it both ways. And any writer of distinction must surely suffer from the fact that his public is limited, the range of his appeal restricted, and the chances of benefiting from informed criticism greatly reduced, all by virtue of the fact that the language he used is so thinly distributed. That this indeed applies to 'Norwegian' in general was something that even Wergeland realized and regretted; that it applies in even greater degree to *Nynorsk* is self-evident, although not everybody will agree with Øverland's estimate when, writing of Duun, he suggested that his appeal was only about a quarter of what it would have been with *Riksmål*.

There is moreover an extra responsibility which this state of affairs imposes on the artist connected with the fact that his personal creativeness not only includes his 'style' but extends also to the very constitution of the language itself. It is only by the courtesy of convention that one can say that Duun and Vesaas write *Nynorsk*; what they in fact write in are languages possessing certain structural qualities in common with the other regional dialects of Norway but incorporating also many of the local characteristics of the speech of Namdal, and West Telemark respectively. The links that bind Duun with Namdal, for example, are both complex and indivisible, with the valley and the fjord supplying not only the milieu of the novels but also the dialect from which Duun draws the linguistic idiosyncrasies of his style. These are works in which the relationship between the 'story' and the medium, between what is said and the language it is said in, is intimate and unbreakable. But the fact that the direct speech of the characters and also the discursive narration of event are conveyed in language that is regionally coloured and vernacular in its inspiration is not all gain; for although these things contribute towards the vividness of style that is such a feature of these novels, it makes any approach to the author by the uninitiated (and incidentally any translation of him) at once more difficult. When therefore an author's language is in great degree his own personal creation, he must take care lest he indulge himself in what becomes more and more a private language. The ultimate terminus of the road he treads is where Stefan George found himself, who when young composed some of his verses in a wholly invented language, presumably so fashioned as to allow the greatest profundity and suppleness of poetic expression for a public that could, by the very nature of things, number no more than one—himself. Both Duun and Vesaas have, therefore, by an accident of linguistic history, each found their authorship occupying some of that problematic territory where linguistics and stylistics overlap. Or, to put it less pretentiously, any fuller account of their styles must inevitably allow into the discussion a disproportionately large amount of essentially linguistic comment.

SELECT BIBLIOGRAPHY OF TRANSLATIONS

PETTER DASS

Nordlands Trompet (publ. 1739)

Fragments of *Trumpet of the North Land* in *Translations from the Norse* by a B.S.S. [member of the British Scandinavian Society, (?) A. Johnston] (Privately printed, Gloucester, ?1879) pp. 65–71.

The Trumpet of Nordland, trans. T. Jorgensen (Northfield, Minnesota, 1954).

LUDVIG HOLBERG

(a) collections

Three Comedies [*Henry and Pernilla, Captain Bombastes Thunderton (Diderich Menschenskræk), Scatterbrains (Den Stundesløse)*], trans. H. W. L. Hime (Longmans Green, London, 1912).

Comedies [*Jeppe of the Hill, The Political Tinker, Erasmus Montanus*] trans. O. J. Campbell and Frederic Schenck (American Scandinavian Foundation, New York, 1914).

Four Plays [*The Fussy Man, The Masked Ladies, The Weather Cock, Masquerades*], trans. Henry Alexander (American Scandinavian Foundation, New York, 1946).

Seven One-Act Plays [*The Talkative Barber (Gert Westphaler), The Arabian Powder, The Christmas Party, Diderich the Terrible, The Peasant in Pawn, Sganarel's Journey to the Land of the Philosophers, The Changed Bridegroom*], trans. Henry Alexander (American Scandinavian Foundation, New York, 1950).

Three Comedies [The Transformed Peasant, The Arabian Powder, The Healing Spring], trans Reginald Spink (Heinemann, London, 1957).

(b) individual works, in versions not included in the above collections

Peder Paars (1719–20).

Extracts in 'Holberg's Peter Paars', trans. anon., in *Dublin University Magazine*, Aug. 1836, 178–189.

Peter Paars, Canto 1, freely trans. [by J. H. Sharman?] from the Danish of Ludwig Holberg (Privately printed, 1862).

Den politiske Kandestøber (1722).

The Blue-apron Statesman, trans. T. Weber (Copenhagen, 1885).

Jeppe paa Bjerget (1723).
   Jeppe on the Hill, trans. Waldemar C. Westergaard (Publ. by the
   Mimer Club of the University of North Dakota, 1906).
Gert Westphaler (1723).
   'The babbling Barber, altered from the Danish,' trans. the Misses
   Corbett (Edinburgh, 1826–27).
Erasmus Montanus (1723).
   Erasmus Montanus, trans. T. Weber (Copenhagen, 1885).
Mascarade (1724).
   The Masquerades, written in imitation of one of Holberg's play
   . . . by F. T. Kühne (Helmstat, 1782)—intended as a text-book for
   use in the teaching of English.
Epistola ad virum perillustrem (1728).
   Memoires of Lewis Holberg, written by himself in Latin and now
   first translated into English (Hunt and Clarke, London, 1827).
Synopsis historiæ universalis (1733).
   An Introduction to Universal History, trans. from the Latin . . . by
   Gregory Sharpe (London, 1755; 2nd ed. 1758; 3rd ed. 1787).
Nicolai Klimii iter subterraneum . . . (1741).
   A Journey to the World Under-Ground, by Nicholas Klimius. Trans.
   from the original (London, 1742; repr. 1746, 1749, 1755); incl. in
   Popular Romances, intro. Henry Weber (Edinburgh, 1812).
   Journey to the World Underground, being the subterraneous travels
   of Niels Klim. From the Latin of Louis Holberg (Th. North,
   London, 1828).
   Niels Klim's Journey under the Ground, trans. John Gierlow (New
   York, 1845).
Moralske Tanker (1744).
   Selected Essays, trans. P. M. Mitchell (Kansas, 1955).

JOHAN SEBASTIAN WELHAVEN

Translations of the poems 'The Republicans' and 'The Fugitive' in
Johan A. Dahl, *Norwegian and Swedish Poems* (Bergen, 1872),
pp. 60–64, 107–112.

HENRIK WERGELAND

Poems, trans. G. M. Gathorne-Hardy, J. Bithell and I. Grøndahl
(London, 1929).
'The Constitution', a poem, in R. G. Latham, *Norway and the Nor-
wegians* (London, 1840), II, pp. 105–107.

'Greeting to England', 'Hardanger' [poems from *The English Pilot*] in J. A. Dahl, *Norwegian and Swedish Poems* (Bergen, 1872).

Part of *The Swallow*, part of *The English Pilot*, and the poem 'To my wallflower', in Edmund Gosse, *Studies in the Literature of Northern Europe* (London, 1879).

Some poems in *Henrik Wergeland, the Norwegian Poet*, with translations by Illit Grøndahl (Newcastle upon Tyne, 1919).

Poems in *Eagle Wings*, with translations by A. G. Dehly (Auburndale, Mass., 1943).

HENRIK IBSEN

(a) collections

The Pillars of Society, and other plays. [*The Pillars of Society*, trans. William Archer; *Ghosts*, trans. William Archer; *An Enemy of Society*, trans. Mrs. Eleanor Marx-Aveling] Introduction by Havelock Ellis. (The Camelot Classics, London, 1888).

Ibsen's Prose Dramas, ed. W. Archer, Authorized English edition. 5 vols. (Walter Scott, London, 1890–91).

vol. 1   *The League of Youth*, trans. W. Archer; *The Pillars of Society*, trans. W. Archer; *A Doll's House*, trans. W. Archer.

vol. 2   *Ghosts*, trans. W. Archer; *An Enemy of the People*, trans. Mrs. Eleanor Marx-Aveling; *The Wild Duck*, trans. Mrs. F. E. Archer.

vol. 3   *Lady Inger of Ostråt*, trans. Charles Archer; *The Vikings at Helgeland*, trans. W. Archer; *The Pretenders*, trans. W. Archer.

vol. 4   *Emperor and Galilean*, trans. W. Archer [based on earlier trans. by Catherine Ray].

vol. 5   *Rosmersholm*, trans. C. Archer; *The Lady from the Sea*, trans. Mrs. F. E. Archer; *Hedda Gabler*, trans. W. Archer.

The Prose Dramas of Henrik Ibsen, ed. Edmund Gosse. Lovell's Series of Foreign Literature. 3 vols. (New York and London, 1890).

vol. 1   *A Doll's House, Pillars of Society, Ghosts*, all trans. W. Archer; *Rosmersholm*, trans. M. Carmichael.

vol. 2   *Lady from the Sea*, trans. Clara Bell; *Enemy of Society*, trans. W. Archer; *The Wild Duck*, trans. Mrs. Eleanor Marx-Aveling; *The Young Men's League*, trans. Henry Carstarphen.

vol. 3   *Hedda Gabler*, trans. William Archer, with preface by E. Gosse.

The Collected Works of Henrik Ibsen. Copyright ed. Revised and edited by William Archer. 12 vols. (Heinemann, London, 1906 ff.).

vol. 1	(1908)	*Lady Inger of Ostråt,* trans. Charles Archer; *The Feast at Solhoug,* trans. W. Archer and Mary Morison; *Love's Comedy,* trans. C. H. Herford.
vol. 2	(1906)	*The Vikings at Helgeland,* trans. W. Archer; *The Pretenders,* trans. W. Archer.
vol. 3	(1906)	*Brand,* trans. C. H. Herford.
vol. 4	(1907)	*Peer Gynt,* trans. W. and C. Archer.
vol. 5	(1907)	*Emperor and Galilean,* trans. W. Archer.
vol. 6	(1906)	*The League of Youth,* trans. W. Archer; *Pillars of Society,* trans. W. Archer.
vol. 7	(1907)	*A Doll's House,* trans. W. Archer; *Ghosts,* trans. W. Archer.
vol. 8	(1907)	*An Enemy of the People,* trans. Mrs. Eleanor Marx-Aveling; *The Wild Duck,* trans. Mrs. F. E. Archer.
vol. 9	(1907)	*Rosmersholm,* trans. C. Archer; *The Lady from the Sea,* trans. Mrs. F. E. Archer.
vol. 10	(1907)	*Hedda Gabler,* trans. Edmund Gosse and W. Archer; *The Master Builder,* trans. E. Gosse and W. Archer.
vol. 11	(1907)	*Little Eyolf,* trans. W. Archer; *John Gabriel Borkman,* trans. W. Archer; *When We Dead Awaken,* trans. W. Archer.
vol. 12	(1912)	*From Ibsen's Workshop.* Notes, scenarios and drafts of modern plays. Trans. A. G. Chater.

Everyman edition of Ibsen (Dent, London, 1910 ff.).

A Doll's House, The Wild Duck [and] *The Lady from the Sea,* trans. R. Farquharson Sharp and Eleanor Marx-Aveling (London, 1910). [The first two dramas trans. Sharp, the last trans. Mrs. Marx-Aveling].

Ghosts, The Warriors at Helgeland [and] *An Enemy of the People,* trans. R. F. Sharp (London, 1911).

The Pretenders, Pillars of Society [and] *Rosmersholm,* trans. R. F. Sharp (London, 1913).

Lady Inger of Ostraat, Love's Comedy [and] *The League of Youth,* trans. R. F. Sharp (London, 1915).

Brand, trans. F. E. Garrett, intro. Philip H. Wicksteed (London, 1915).

Peer Gynt, trans. R. F. Sharp (London, 1921).

Early Plays [*Catiline, The Warrior's Barrow, Olaf Liljekrans*], trans. Anders Orbeck (American Scandinavian Foundation, New York, 1921).

Three Plays [*The Pillars of the Community, The Wild Duck, Hedda Gabler*]; *The Master Builder and other plays* [*Rosmersholm, Little Eyolf, John Gabriel Borkman*], trans. Una Ellis-Fermor (Penguin, London, 1950 and 1958).

Six Plays [*A Doll's House, Ghosts, An Enemy of the People, Rosmersholm, Hedda Gabler, The Master Builder*], trans. Eva le Gallienne (New York, 1957).

(b) individual works, in versions not represented in the collections listed above

Catilina (1850): Translation of Act I in *Translations from the Norse*, by a B.S.S. [member of the British Scandinavian Society, (?) A. Johnston] (Privately printed, Gloucester, ?1879).

Brand (1866): *Brand*, trans. into English prose by W. Wilson [i.e. More Adey] (London, 1891); *Brand*, trans. into English prose by J. M. Olberman (Oregon, 1912); *Brand*, trans. into English verse, rhymed and in the original metre, by Miles Menander Dawson (Four Seas, U.S.A., 1916); *Brand*, trans. James Forsyth in collaboration with Evelyn Ramsden, perf. BBC, December 1949, unpublished; *Brand* trans. Michael Meyer, perf. Lyric, Hammersmith, May 1959, unpublished.

Peer Gynt (1867): *The Fantasy of Peer Gynt*, selections . . . done into English verse by Isabelle M. Pagan (Theosophical Pub. Co., London, 1909); *Peer Gynt*, trans. R. Ellis Roberts (London, 1913); *Peer Gynt*, trans. G. Hult (New York, 1933); *Peer Gynt*, English version by Norman Ginsbury (London, 1946); *Peer Gynt*, American version by Paul Green (New York, 1951); *Peer Gynt*, trans. Horace Maynard Finney (New York, 1955).

Kejser og Galilæer (1873): *The Emperor and the Galilean*, trans. Catharine Ray (London, 1876).

Samfundets støtter (1877): 'The Supports of Society', a 'hurried' translation made by William Archer in 1878, which 'no publisher would look at'; extracts, together with an analysis, in W. Archer, 'Henrik Ibsen's New Drama', in *Mirror of Literature*, 2 March 1878; 'Quicksands', unpub. trans. by W. Archer, prod. at Gaiety Theatre, 15 December 1880.

Et dukkehjem (1879): *Nora*, trans. T. Weber (Copenhagen, 1880); *Nora*, trans. Henrietta Frances Lord (London, 1882); 'Breaking a

Butterfly', adaptation by Henry Arthur Jones and Henry Herman, prod. Prince's Theatre, 3 March 1884, unpublished; *A Doll's House*, English version by Norman Ginsbury (London, 1950).

Gengangere (1881): 'Ghosts', trans. Henrietta Frances Lord, in *Today*, 1885, pp. 29, 65, 105 ff.; *Ghosts*, trans. Norman Ginsbury (London, 1938); *Ghosts*, trans. Bjorn Koefoed (New York, 1952).

En Folkefiende (1882): *An Enemy of the People*, trans. Jenny Covan (London, 1924); *An Enemy of the People*, English version by Norman Ginsbury (London, 1940); *An Enemy of the People*, an adaptation by Arthur Miller (New York, 1951).

Vildanden (1884): *The Wild Duck*, trans. Max Faber (Heinemann, London, 1958).

Rosmersholm (1886): *Rosmersholm*, trans. Louis N. Parker (London, [1889]).

Hedda Gabler (1890): *Hedda Gabler*, trans. Edmund Gosse (London, 1891).

Bygmester Solness (1892): *The Master Builder*, trans. Jno W. Arctander (Minneapolis, 1893).

Lille Eyolf (1894): 'Little Eyolf', trans. Michael Meyer, perf. BBC February 1956, prod. at Lyric, Hammersmith, March 1958, unpublished.

John Gabriel Borkman (1896): trans. Michael Meyer, perf. ITV Nov. 1958, unpublished.

(c) poems, etc.

'Terje Vigen' trans. J. A. Dahl, in *Norwegian and Swedish Poems* (Bergen, 1872).

Several poems trans. Edmund Gosse, in *On Viol and Flute* (London, 1873).

Terje Vigen, three shorter poems, etc. in *Translations from the Norse*, by a B.S.S. [member of British Scandinavian Society (?) A. Johnston] (Privately printed, Gloucester, ?1879).

Gleanings from Ibsen, selected and edited E. A. Keddell and P. C. Standing (London, 1897).

Lyrical Poems, trans. R. A. Streatfield (London, 1902).

On the Heights [trans. of *Paa vidderne*] trans. W. N. Guthrie (Tennessee, 1910).

Lyrics and Poems, trans. F. E. Garrett (London, 1912).

Terje Vigen, trans. D. Svennungsen (Minneapolis, 1923).

Terje Vigen, trans. A. G. Dehly (Auburndale, Mass., 1938).

In the Mountain Wilderness, and other poems, trans. T. Jorgenson (Northfield, Minn., 1957).

(d) letters, speeches, etc.

Correspondence, trans. and ed. by Mary Morison (London, 1905).

Speeches and new letters, trans. Arne Kildal (Boston, U.S.A., 1910).

BJØRNSTJERNE BJØRNSON

(a) collections

Life by the fells and fiords. A Norwegian sketch book. Trans. A. Plesner and S. Rugeley Powers (London [1879])—includes *Arne*, *Bridal March*, eleven other stories and six poems.

Novels, trans. Rasmus B. Anderson (Boston, U.S.A., 1881–83). 7 vols. Synnøve Solbakken. Arne. A Happy Boy. The Bridal March. The Fisher Maiden. Captain Mansana. Magnhild.

The Novels of Bjørnstjerne Bjørnson, edited by Edmund Gosse (Heinemann, London, 1895–1909), 13 volumes. 1. *Synnøve Solbakken*; 2. *Arne*; 3. *A Happy Boy*; 4. *The Fisher Lass*; 5. *The Bridal March, One Day*; 6. *Magnhild, Dust*; 7. *Captain Mansana, Mother's Hands*; 8. *Absalom's Hair, A Painful Memory*; 9, 10. *In God's Way*; 11, 12. *The Heritage of the Kurts*; 13. *Mary*.

Peasant Stories, trans. C. E. Nordberg (Minneapolis, 1920).

Three Comedies [*The Newly-married Couple, Leonarda, A Gauntlet*], trans. R. Farquharson Sharp (Everyman, Dent, London, 1912).

Three Dramas [*The Editor, The Bankrupt, The King*], trans. R. Farquharson Sharp (Everyman, Dent, London, 1914).

Plays: first series [*The Gauntlet, Beyond Our Power, The New System*], trans. Edwin Björkman (Duckworth, London, 1913).

Plays: second series [*Love and Geography, Beyond Human Might, Laboremus*], trans. Edwin Björkman (Duckworth, London, 1913).

(b) individual works

Synnøve Solbakken (1857): *Trust and Trial.* A story from the Danish by Mary Howitt (London, 1858); *Love and Life in Norway*, trans. the Hon. Augusta Bethell and Augusta Plesner (London, 1877); *Synnøve Solbakken*, trans. Julie Sutter (London, 1881)—repr. Gosse ed., vol. 1; *Sunny Hill*, intro. Annie S. Cutter (New York, 1932).

Halte Hulda (1858): Extracts trans. H. H. Boyesen, in 'B.B. as a dramatist', *North American Review*, vol. 116 (Boston, 1873), 109–138.

Arne (1858): *Arne, or peasant life in Norway*, trans. by 'a Norwegian' [Thomas Krag] (Bergen [1861]); *Arne*, trans. Augusta Plesner and S. Rugeley Powers (London, 1866); *Arne. The Fisher Lassie*, trans. Walter Low (London, 1890)—repr. Gosse ed., vol. 2.

En glad gut (1860): *Ovind*, trans. Sivert and Elizabeth Hjerleid (London, 1869); *The Happy Boy*, trans. by H. R. G. (Boston, 1870); *The Happy Lad*, from the Norwegian (London, [1882]); *A Happy Boy*, trans. Mrs. W. Archer (London, 1896)—Gosse ed., vol. 3.

Sigurd Slembe (1862): *Sigurd Slembe*, trans. William Morton Payne (Chicago, 1910).

Maria Stuart i Skotland (1864): *Mary, Queen of Scots*, trans. Clemens Peterson (Chicago, 1897); *Mary, Queen of Scots*, trans. A. Sahlberg (Chicago, 1912).

De Nygifte (1865): *The Newly-married Couple*, trans. Theodor Soelfeldt (London, 1868); *Love in Wedlock*, trans. W. and C. Wilkinson (Printed for the translators, Lowestoft, 1869); *The Newly-married Couple*, trans. S. and E. Hjerleid (London, 1870); *A Lesson in Marriage*, trans. Grace Isabel Colbron (New York, 1910).

Fiskerjenten (1868): *The Fisher-maiden*, from the Author's German (*sic*) edition, by M. E. Niles (New York, 1869); *The Fisher Girl*, trans. Sivert and Elizabeth Hjerleid (London, 1871); *The Fishing Girl*, trans. Augusta Plesner and Frederika Richardson (London, 1877); see also *Arne* . . . trans. Walter Low.

Digte og Sange (1870): *Poems and Songs*, trans. . . . . in the original metres by Arthur Hubbell Palmer (New York, 1915).

Arnljot Gelline (1870): *Arnljot Gelline*, trans. William Morton Payne (New York, 1917).

Brude-Slaatten (1872): *The Bridal March*, trans. J. Evan Williams (London, 1893).

En handske (1883): *A Gauntlet* ,trans. H. L. Brækstad (London [1890]); 'A glove', trans. Thyge Sögård, in *Poet Lore* (Philadelphia, 1892); *A Gauntlet*, trans. Osman Edwards (London, 1894).

Over Ævne I (1883): *Pastor Sang*, trans. William Wilson [i.e. More Adey], with frontispiece by Aubrey Beardsley and cover by Aymer Vallance (London, 1893).

Det flager i byen og på havnen (1884): *The Heritage of the Kurts*, trans. Cecil Fairfax (London, 1892)—repr. Gosse ed., vols. 11, 12.

Paa Guds veje (1889): *In God's Way*, trans. Elizabeth Carmichael (London, 1890)—repr. Gosse ed., vols. 9, 10.

Paul Lange og Tora Parsberg (1898): *Paul Lange and Tora Parsberg*, trans. H. L. Brækstad (London, 1899).

Laboremus (1901): *Laboremus* [translator not named] (London, 1901); 'Laboremus' in *Fortnightly Review*, vol. 69, May 1901, lit. sup.

Mary (1906): *Mary*, trans. Mary Morison (London, 1909)—repr. Gosse ed., vol. 13.

Når den ny vin blomstrer (1909): 'When the new wine blooms', trans. Lee M. Hollander, in *Poet Lore*, vol. 22 (Boston, 1911), 1–69.

ALEXANDER KIELLAND

Garman & Worse (1880): *Garman and Worse*, trans. W. W. Kettlewell (London, 1885).

Else (1881): *Elsie: a Christmas story*, trans. Miles Menander Dawson (Chicago, 1894).

Skipper Worse, trans. Henry John, Earl of Ducie (London, 1885).

Sne (1886): the second chapter of *Snow*, trans. Henry John, Earl of Ducie (Gloucester [1887]).

Omkring Napoleon (1905): *Napoleon's men and methods*, trans. Joseph McCabe (London [1907]).

Various short stories in: *Tales of Two Countries*, trans. William Archer (London, 1891); *Norse Tales and Sketches*, trans. R. L. Cassie (London, 1896); 'The battle of Waterloo', in John Fulford Vicary, *A Stork's Nest, or pleasant reading from the North* (London, 1887); 'Siesta', in *Modern Ghosts*, intro. George William Curtis (New York, 1890).

JONAS LIE

Den Fremsynte (1870): Extracts from 'The Visionary', trans. Mrs. Ellis, in Mark Antony Lower, *Wayside Notes in Scandinavia* (London, 1874); *The Visionary, or Pictures from Nordland*, trans. Jessie Muir (London, 1894).

Tremasteren 'Fremtiden' (1872): *The Barque 'Future': or, Life in the far North*, trans. Mrs. Ole Bull (Chicago, 1879).

Lodsen og hans Hustru (1874): *A Norse love story: the pilot and his wife*, trans. Mrs. Ole Bull (Chicago, 1876); *The Pilot and his Wife*, trans. G. L. Tottenham (London, 1877).

Livsslaven (1883): *One of Life's Slaves*, trans. Jessie Muir (London, 1895).

Familjen paa Gilje (1883): *The Family at Gilje*, trans. Samuel Coffin Eastman (New York, 1920).

Kommandørens Døtre (1886): *The Commodore's Daughters*, trans. H. L. Brækstad and Gertrude Hughes (London, 1892).

Trold (1891): *Weird Tales from Northern Seas*, trans. R. Nisbet Bain (London, 1893).

Niobe (1893): *Niobe*, trans. H. L. Brækstad (London, 1897).

Miscellaneous: *Little Grey, the pony of Nordfjord*, trans. the Hon.

Mrs. Arbuthnott (née Douglas) (Edinburgh, 1873); 'The North-fjord Horse', trans. Nellie V. Anderson, in *Scandinavia*, II (Chicago, 1885), 233–37, 260–64; 'The Life Convict' [beginning of *Livsslaven*], trans. J. Langland, in *Scandinavia*, III (Chicago, 1886), 16–19.

SIGBJØRN OBSTFELDER

Poems, trans. P. Selver, Norwegian and English, Sheldonian series, no. 6 (Oxford, 1920).

KNUT HAMSUN

Sult (1890): *Hunger*, trans. George Egerton [pseu. for Mary C. Dunne, later Mrs. Egerton Clairmonte, later Mrs. Golding Bright] (London, 1899).

Mysterier (1892): *Mysteries*, trans. A. G. Chater (London, 1927).

Ny Jord (1893): *Shallow Soil*, trans. C. C. Hyllested (London, 1914).

Pan (1894): *Pan*, trans. W. W. Worster (London, 1920); *Pan*, trans. J. W. McFarlane (London, 1955).

Victoria (1898): *Victoria*, trans. A. G. Chater (London, 1923).

Sværmere (1904): *Mothwise*, trans. W. W. Worster (London, 1921).

Under Høststjærnen (1906): 'Under the Autumn Star', in *Wanderers*, trans. W. W. Worster (London, 1922).

Benoni (1907): *Benoni*, trans. A. G. Chater (New York, 1925).

Rosa (1908): *Rosa*, trans. A. G. Chater (New York, 1926).

En Vandrer spiller med Sordin (1909): 'With Muted Strings', in *Wanderers*, trans. W. W. Worster (London, 1922).

Den sidste Glæde (1911): *Look back on Happiness*, trans. P. Wiking (New York, 1940).

Livet i Vold (1910): *In the Grip of Life*, trans. Graham and Tristan Rawson (London, 1924).

Børn av Tiden (1913): *Children of the Age*, trans. J. S. Scott (London, 1924).

Segelfoss By (1915): *Segelfoss Town*, trans. J. S. Scott (London, 1925).

Markens Grøde (1917): *Growth of the Soil*, trans. W. W. Worster (London, 1920).

Konerne ved Vandposten (1920): *The Women at the Pump*, trans. A. G. Chater (London, 1928).

Siste Kapitel (1923): *Chapter the Last*, trans. A. G. Chater (London, 1929).

Landstrykere (1927): *Vagabonds*, trans. Eugene Gay-Tifft (London, 1931).

August (1930): *August*, trans. Eugene Gay-Tifft (London, 1932).

Men Livet lever (1933): *The Road Leads On*, trans. Eugene Gay-Tifft (London, 1935).

Ringen sluttet (1936): *The Ring is Closed*, trans. Eugene Gay-Tifft (New York, 1937).

SIGRID UNDSET

Fortællingen om Viga-Ljot og Vigdis (1909): *Gunnar's Daughter*, trans. A. G. Chater (London, 1936).

Jenny (1911): *Jenny*, trans. A. Gripenwald (London, 1920).

Splinten av troldspeilet (1917): *Images in a Mirror*, trans. A. G. Chater (London, 1938).

Kristin Lavransdatter (1920–22): *Kristin Lavransdatter*, trans. C. Archer and J. S. Scott (New York, 1923–27).

Olav Audunssön (1925–27): *The Master of Hestviken*, trans. A. G. Chater (London, 1928–30).

Gymnadenia (1929): *The Wild Orchid*, trans. A. G. Chater (New York, 1931).

Den brændende busk (1930): *The Burning Bush*, trans. A. G. Chater (New York, 1932).

Ida Elisabeth (1932): *Ida Elisabeth*, trans. A. G. Chater (London, 1933).

Etapper (1929, 1933): *Stages on the Road*, trans. A. G. Chater (New York, 1934).

Elleve aar (1934): *The Longest Years*, trans. A. G. Chater (London, 1935).

Den trofaste hustru (1936): *The Faithful Wife*, trans. A. G. Chater (London, 1937).

Norske Helgener (1937): *Saga of Saints*, trans. from MS. by E. C. Ramsden (London, 1934).

Selvportretter og landskapsbilleder (1938): *Men, women and places*, trans. A. G. Chater (New York, 1939).

Madame Dorthea (1939): *Madame Dorthea*, trans. A. G. Chater (London, 1941).

Miscellaneous: *Happy Times in Norway*, trans. from the Norwegian MS. by Joran Birkeland (London, 1943); *Return to the Future*, trans. from the Norwegian MS. by H. C. K. Næseth (London, 1943); *Christmas and Twelfth Night*, trans. E. C. Ramsden (London, 1932).

ARNE GARBORG

Fred (1892): *Peace*, trans. P. D. Carleton (New York, 1929).
Den burtkomne faderen (1899): *The Lost Father*, trans. M. J. Leland (Boston, 1920).

OLAV DUUN

Det gode samvite (1916): *Good Conscience*, trans. Edwin Björkman (London, 1928).
Juvikfolke (1918–23): *The People of Juvik*, trans. A. G. Chater (New York, 1930–35)—vol. 1, *The Trough of the Wave*; vol. 2, *The Blind Man*; vol. 3, *The Big Wedding*; vol. 4, *Odin in Fairyland*; vol. 5, *Odin Grows Up*; vol. 6, *The Storm*.

INDEX

Book titles in Norwegian carry only the reference to the page where the original title is printed alongside its English equivalent; where other references to the work occur, they are to be found against the English title, thus: *Vildanden*, 55; *Wild Duck, The*, 55, 62, 67 . . . etc.
The Norwegian letters *å* and *æ* are listed under *a*, and *ø* under *o*.